The Ministry Marathon

The
Ministry
Marathon

**CARING FOR YOURSELF WHILE YOU CARE
FOR THE PEOPLE OF GOD**

Tim Wright
with Vignettes by Lori Woods

ABINGDON PRESS/Nashville

THE MINISTRY MARATHON
CARING FOR YOURSELF WHILE YOU CARE FOR THE PEOPLE OF GOD

Copyright © 1999 by Abingdon Press

This book is printed on acid-free paper.

Library of Congress Cataloging-in-Publication Data

Wright, Tim, 1957–
    The ministry marathon : caring for yourself while you care for the people of God / Tim Wright & Lori Woods.
        p.   cm.
    ISBN 0-687-02435-8 (alk. paper)
    1. Clergy—Religious life.   2. Clergy—Conduct of life.
I. Woods, Lori, 1963–   .   II. Title.
BV4011.6.W75   1999
248.8892—dc21   99-31671
                                                                                CIP

Scripture quotations noted NRSV are taken from the New Revised Standard Version of the Bible. Copyright © 1989 by the Division of Christian Education of the National Council of the Churches of Christ in the United States of America. Used by permission.

Those noted NIV are from the Holy Bible: New International Version. Copyright © 1973, 1978, 1984 by the International Bible Society. Used by permission of Zondervan Bible Publishers.

Those noted CEV are from the New Testament of the Contemporary English Version. Copyright © 1995 by The American Bible Society. Used by permission of Thomas Nelson Publishers.

99 00 01 02 03 04 05 06 07 08—10 9 8 7 6 5 4 3 2 1

MANUFACTURED IN THE UNITED STATES OF AMERICA

TO

Jeff, Dave, JoAnn, Jan, Alycia, and Mike

for cheering me on through the marathon.
—Tim

TO

Ashli, Kassi, and Jacob;

I love you.
—Lori

Training Tips for the Ministry Marathon

Let the Race Begin

Walt Disney World, January 1997

I've been awake since midnight, and am lucky if I slept three hours. For the past several hours I've been lying in bed thinking about what I'm about to do—run my first, and probably last, marathon. I've been training, with starts and stops, for two years and have worked hard to get to this point, battling through doubt, injury, stiffness, and fatigue. And now, when I probably need it the most, I'm too excited to sleep. I hope that my adrenaline will keep me going throughout the race.

At 3:00 A.M., I roll out of bed and begin to prepare for the run. I get dressed, eat a banana and bagel, and start drinking lots of water. This means several trips to the bathroom. I stretch out, then talk to my wife, who's still in bed but excited for me nonetheless. My kids are sound asleep in the next room.

At 5:00 A.M., I head to the main lobby of the hotel and meet my two brothers, both veterans of several marathons. They have kindly consented to run at my very slow pace. We drive to the EPCOT parking lot, the starting and finishing point of this 26.2-mile race. As I stand in line for the portable toilet, the woman behind me talks of how she slept for only an hour. This is her first marathon, too.

At 5:45 A.M., we head to the starting line. Because I'll be running the marathon between four and a half and five hours, we move toward the back of the pack. A quick run to the bushes and I'm ready. I can feel the energy building. Suddenly the music begins to play. Fireworks go off. I yell out an uncontrollable "Yes!" as slowly the pack begins to inch forward. It takes almost three minutes to actually get to the starting line. But I finally cross it and begin one of the most invigorating, challenging, grueling, inspiring, and rewarding journeys of my life.

Minneapolis, March 1984

It's a blizzard outside. Inside the church is almost empty. Only my closest friends and family members are willing to brave the weather to participate in my ordination. In fact, my in-laws almost don't make it because of the treacherous roads.

Three pastors—my soon-to-be partner in ministry, my grandfather, and my parents' pastor—pray for me through the laying on of hands. As I kneel at the altar my brother sings a song about dying to self, as Jesus lives in us. While he sings, I think about what's happening to me. I am becoming a real pastor!

I've dreamed about this experience almost all of my life, since second grade. And from that time on, my whole life has been geared toward ministry. Years of training have gone into this moment. I have a hard time keeping in my emotions as I think about the privilege and responsibility of ordination. As I kneel at the altar I know I am embarking on one of the most invigorating, challenging, grueling, inspiring, and rewarding journeys of my life.

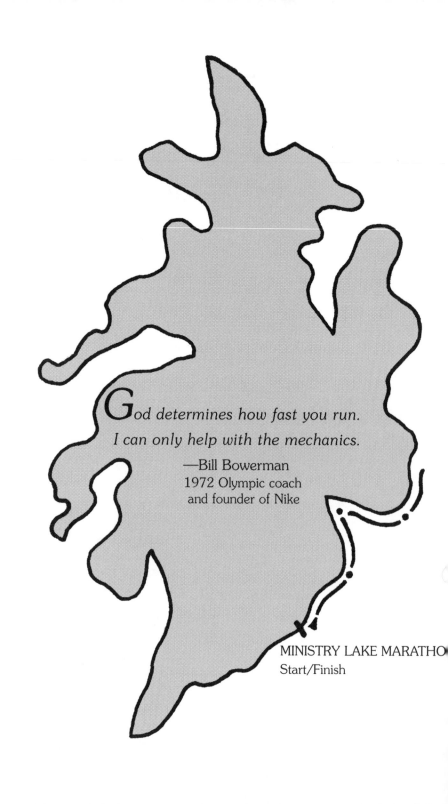

*God determines how fast you run.
I can only help with the mechanics.*

—Bill Bowerman
1972 Olympic coach
and founder of Nike

MINISTRY LAKE MARATHON
Start/Finish

Running on Empty

We must be determined to run the race that is
ahead of us.
—Hebrews 12:1c CEV

*Jesus was walking along the road one day when he
came upon a man crying. "Friend," Jesus asked, "what's
wrong?"*

*The man replied, "I'm blind. Can you help me see?"
Jesus reached out his hand and healed him.*

*As Jesus continued on his way he came across a woman
weeping. "Friend," Jesus asked, "what's wrong?"*

*The woman answered, "I'm lame and can't walk. Can
you help me?" Jesus reached out his hand and healed her.*

*As he moved on Jesus came upon another man sob-
bing. "Friend," Jesus asked, "what's wrong?"*

*The man replied, "I'm a minister. Can you help me?"
And Jesus sat down and wept with him.*

> **Sprint:** To run at top speed,
> especially for a short distance.

A few years ago a survey of pastors revealed the following:

- Ninety percent work more than forty-six hours per week.
- Eighty percent feel that pastoral ministry is negatively affecting their families.
- Seventy-five percent reported a significant crisis due to stress at least once in their ministry.
- Seventy percent do not have someone they consider a close friend.
- Seventy percent say their self-image is lower since entering the ministry.

One management guru claims that pastors are the most discouraged professionals, period.

Every year at the end of my church's national evangelism conference, we offer individual prayer for each participant. Year after year, pastors and church leaders pour out their hurts, their disappointments, and their discouragement. With tears and deep sighs they tell of their broken hearts and shattered hopes.

All across the United States and around the world, a growing number of church leaders, both paid and non-paid, find themselves facing painful personal issues as a result of ministry. Many have lost their passion for mission and the gospel. Their dreams of significant ministry have crumbled beyond recognition. The challenges and stresses of ministry have drained them of energy and joy. They've burned out. To use the language of the marathon, they've "hit the wall," that invisible barrier that leaves them depleted of the will to go on, that leads them to give up.

The reasons for such discouragement are varied and many: conflict, tight budgets, power issues, church decline, family struggles, and a lack of solid relationships, to name a few. Part of the reason, however, has to do with the way we as leaders care for ourselves. Ministry, by its very nature, demands a great deal of our time and personal investment. The needs of others tend to set the tone for each day. As a result, we often find it difficult to squeeze in time to focus on our own lives. We race from one meeting to the next, from crisis to hospital call, from sermon preparation to denominationally sponsored events. And we barely have the chance to take a breath. We're continually sprinting through the day, but the sprint never ends. Eventually we wind up running on empty. We begin to feel the stress mentally, emotionally, physically, and spiritually. Some of us are so exhausted, in fact, that we're ready to give up.

> **Marathon:** A long distance race;
> an endurance test.

In 1995 I decided to run a marathon (26.2 miles), a dream I'd had for years. Unfortunately, due to a back injury eight years earlier, I had all but given up on that dream. But with my fortieth birthday looming on the horizon, I de-cided I wanted to give the marathon a shot. (Oh, what we'll do under the banner of "midlife.") So, on January 5, 1997, I ran the Walt Disney World Marathon. The race took me four hours, fifty-four minutes, and seventeen seconds. But my time isn't the point. The point is that I finished the race. It took me two years of training filled with breathtaking runs, nagging injuries, and lots of pasta—but I did it. In the end, while at times the training was tiring and wearing, taking on the marathon was worth it. Running that marathon was one of the greatest experiences of my life.

During those two years of training, and during the race itself, I learned some things about caring for myself that have a lot to say about thriving in ministry. For example, I learned in a new way that a *sprint* differs radically from a *marathon*. A sprint musters all of its energy for a quick burst of speed over a short distance for a short period of time. A marathon, on the other hand, slows down and conserves energy for the long haul.

Many of us approach ministry as if it were a sprint. We run at full speed all day long. But "ministry sprinters" know from experience that we simply can't expend that kind of energy day after day without burning out. God didn't wire us that way. So to thrive and survive in ministry, we need to approach it like a marathon—to develop the skills that will help us conserve our energy, using bursts of it for certain occasions, then replenishing it for the next burst. In marathoning endurance, not speed, is the crucial issue.

I also learned that you can't simply *try* to run a marathon. I couldn't sign up for the race on race day, lace up a pair of shoes, and run it without training. I would have killed myself. To run a marathon, one must train for it—conditioning the body, mind, and spirit for the challenge. The same holds true for ministry. We need to *train* ourselves mentally, emotionally, physically, and spiritually so that we can stay in the race—especially in the low-energy times. In life and ministry, training makes all of the difference, because training builds in us life-saving habits. Training gets us and keeps us in shape for the demands, joys, and challenges of mission.

My Reason for Writing

I'm often asked during speaking events how leaders can keep up their energy level in the midst of a busy and demanding ministry. The question has been raised so much lately (especially by middle-aged boomers) that I felt it was time to put some thoughts to computer.

In addition, I write out of recent personal experience. Ironically, while working on this book I have experienced the toughest year of my fifteen-year ministry. The past several months have been filled with difficult staffing situations, my turning forty, our church's moving from one campus to another and all of the chaos that goes with it, and the near loss of my dad to a major heart attack. In my journal I write of moments in which I've questioned my call, my passion, and my willingness to keep at it. At times it frightened me so much that I wondered if I'd ever get back on track. Ministry simply wasn't fun anymore. After fourteen years of absolutely loving ministry, the thought of not enjoying it scared me. I'd "hit the wall."

I'm convinced that the tips in this book helped me out of the hole. Over the years these tips had become habits for me—habits that I practiced even when I didn't feel like doing so. And they pulled me through "the wall."

Finally, I write as one who loves pastors and church workers and believes that the call to ministry is an awesome privilege. My heart breaks when I hear of burned-out, frustrated Christian leaders. I want to see pastors and church leaders rediscover their own importance and value to God—to rediscover what a special gift they are—and how vital it is that they take time to care for themselves so that they can lead others. Perhaps this book can be one tool among many to help encourage and support those called to the task of sharing the gospel through public ministry.

With that in mind, the following pages offer some advice for running the marathon of ministry—eight training tips that can help put the passion, energy, joy, and enthusiasm back into ministry and help leaders either run through "the wall" or avoid it altogether:

Massage Your Mind
Adjust Your Attitude
Replenish Your Resources
Affirm Your Affections
Track Your Time
Hone Your Heart
Own Up to Others
Nurture Your Nature

While training is never easy, it does transform our lives and gets us into shape for dynamic, exciting ministry and mission. So I invite you to lace up your running shoes and join me for a training experience that can reenergize your life and recharge your ministry. Step 1 is a page turn away.

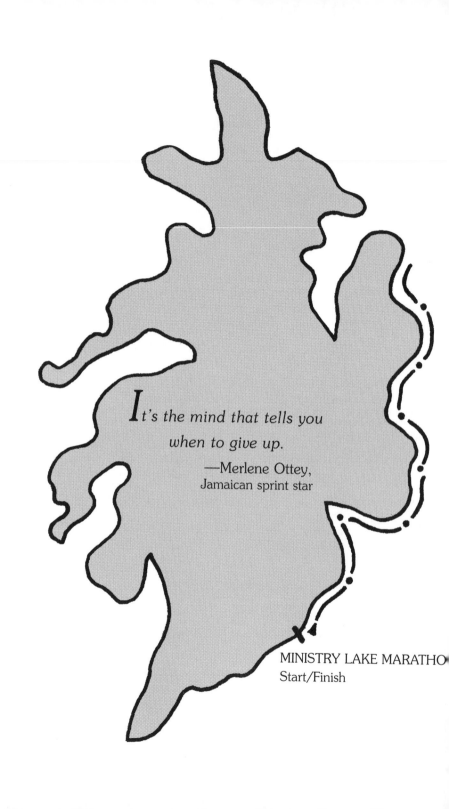

It's the mind that tells you when to give up.

—Merlene Ottey,
Jamaican sprint star

MINISTRY LAKE MARATHON
Start/Finish

Training Tip #1
Massage Your Mind

Be transformed by the renewing of your minds.
—Romans 12:2b NRSV

Another church council meeting. All she had to do was make it through this one meeting and she would have a couple of days with no meetings whatsoever.

"Oh sure. You know that every time you schedule a 'No Meeting Day' somehow one tends to sneak up on you. Church has a life of its own, you know."

"Yeah, I know. Now stop it! I'm trying to listen."

Lately it seemed that every time Beth tried to concentrate on one thing, her brain decided to focus on something else. More and more she was having these internal conversations.

Glancing at her watch, she saw the time creeping toward 11:00 p.m. Jacob, president and principal mouthpiece of the church council, had been droning on for over an hour about . . . What was he droning on about?

21

Beth, the well-loved pastor of Grace Lutheran Church, began racking her brain trying to remember what this council meeting was about. Her eyelids felt heavy and her head began to throb at the temple near her blonde hair.

"Mom always thought my hair looked like a halo."

"Now stop that!" Beth chastened herself, not really knowing if the rest of the council members heard the voice in her head. She caught a flicker of a grin cross Mark's face, and she knew she had unconsciously spoken what only her mind was to have heard.

"I'm sorry, Jacob. My mind wandered momentarily. I'm with you now, though. Please continue."

Mark grinned again. Mark and his wife were great friends to Beth and her husband. Fortunately, Mark understood her hectic life as a pastor and how at times, as a result, her mind turned to mush when she was tired.

"It's good to have friends. . . . We really need to have Mark and Cindy over soon," said the voice in Beth's head.

"Oh, yeah. That's all you need. Another engagement."

"Well, it wouldn't really be an engagement. We'd be with friends."

"Oh, great. Now I'm arguing with my own brain. I wonder if it's the left brain taking on the right brain or vice versa?"

"Well, it really doesn't matter because Jacob is trying to get your attention."

And then, as if from out of a fog, the voice became clearer. "Pastor, we're ready to vote on this issue. Are you in agreement?"

"Well, um, Jacob, maybe you could quickly review for me—uh, us—exactly what we're voting on again, just so we're all clear on the issue."

Groans rose from every council member except Mark. He merely chuckled.

And, knowing exactly what her own brain was going to tell her at that precise moment, Beth quickly told both the left and right sides of her brain to keep their opinions to themselves.

When she arrived home late that night, she found the house quiet. Tom, her husband of twelve years, would have gone to bed hours ago. Slipping quietly into their room, she discovered that Tom had left the light on for her and he was still awake.

"How was your meeting?"

"Oh, you know. The same old same old."

"Mind wandered again, huh?"

"Tom, you know me far too well. I sure hope God reveals to me in a dream tonight what it was that the council and I unanimously voted to pass this evening. I could be in big trouble."

"Good night, Sweetheart. Sweet dreams."

"Cute."

Maybe she'll call Mark in the morning and try to pry some information out of him. Oh, it's good to have friends on the church council. And with that thought, she fell asleep.

Marathon training, like other forms of exercise, offers the body, mind, and spirit all sorts of life-enhancing benefits, including new levels of energy, clearer thinking, a better night's sleep,

Training Log: November 21.

Ran for thirty minutes today. My mind seemed to be in neutral. A wonderful, refreshing, invigorating run.

a healthy heart, and so on. But marathon training and the race itself can also add stress that can fatigue and injure the body if not dealt with properly.

As the date for the Walt Disney World Marathon grew closer, I felt my body desperately needing something to work out the knots and reenergize it, something that would help my body relax and recuperate from the stress. To my absolute delight I found that special something—*massage therapy.*

Now I'm not the type who likes a lot of touchy-feely stuff, but I found the touch of massage therapy revitalizing and, to be honest, marathon-saving. I'm not sure I could have run the marathon were it not for the healing touch of massage. In the hands of a skilled, licensed therapist the stiffness loosened up and the knots untied themselves. After each session, my body was ready once again to meet the challenge of training. As I learned again and again, marathons are won and lost on the basis of the kind of care and rest we offer our bodies.

Ministry training can have similar effects on us. As we train for and run the ministry marathon we often find ourselves stressed out, bruised, and battered. This is particularly true of our minds, the primary muscle used in ministry. So much of ministry is spiritual, mental, and emotional. Each day our mind gets a workout unlike that of most professionals. So from time to time it needs something to knead out the knots, ease the stiffness, and reenergize it for the next event. That special something is mind massage—what the Bible calls the renewing of the mind.

Massage Benefits

Massage offers the following benefits to both the body and mind. It

- improves circulation and relieves congestion.
- calms the mind.
- promotes emotional balance and a sense of well-being.
- sets up conditions for the body to heal itself.
- helps to prevent stiffness after exercise.
- relieves tension, stress, and anxiety.
- helps overcome fatigue.
- improves muscle tone.

Massaging our minds keeps us fresh, energized, and focused for the long haul. It stimulates our creativity and releases the body's built-in ability to stretch beyond what we think is possible—ingredients necessary for running the marathon of ministry.

Mind Massage Techniques

Mind massage can take on many different forms. Listed below are a few ideas to get you started.

1. Massage your mind with God's forgiveness. In the movie *City Slickers,* Phil shares with his friends the belief that he's going nowhere. He's messed up too many times. He's completely wasted his life. With tears in his eyes he buries his head in Mitch's shoulder and weeps.

Mitch hugs him for a moment and says, "Phil, remember when we were kids and we used to play ball? And the ball would get stuck in the tree and we'd yell, 'Do over!' Well, Phil, your life is a 'do over.' You get a clean slate."

Phil stares at him for a moment and replies, "I have no place to live. I'm going to be wiped out in a divorce because I committed adultery. I probably won't be able to see my kids. I'm alone. How does that slate look now?"

As pastors and Christian leaders, we delight in telling others that the slate is clean, that because of Jesus they get a "do over" every day. But we don't always hear and internalize that message ourselves. Many of us, being perfectionists, can offer forgiveness, but we have a hard time receiving it. Like Phil, we see the scratches and failures marring the slate. We remember the missteps of ministry, the wrong decisions, the failure to call on a dying member, the hurtful words spoken to a fellow volunteer. And we continually beat ourselves up over it.

The truth is, we need to have our minds immersed in the love and forgiveness of Jesus just as much as our church members do. We need to let the unconditional acceptance of Jesus massage out the guilt and shame and reenergize us with hope. Every day we need a fresh touch of his grace to rejuvenate our battered minds so that we can continue the race set before us. Filling our minds with Bible verses, songs, and hymns about God's forgiveness massages the mind and keeps it healthy for life and ministry. Hearing from a trusted friend a good word of forgiveness lightens the stress and improves the mind's capacity for action. A daily mind massage with God's forgiveness gets us back into the race.

2. Knead out the knots through a commitment to learning. Great leaders make a commitment to ongoing learning. They never stop asking questions and digging for the answers that will help them grow personally and professionally. Conferences, books, conversations, and online chat rooms help energize the mind—working out the stiffness, stretching the mind, and keeping it healthy.

3. Stimulate the mind by using your God-given imagination. When Frank Lloyd Wright was nine years old, his uncle, a quiet, no-nonsense man, took him for a walk through a snow-covered field. When they reached the other side, his uncle pointed out the tracks they had made in the snow. The uncle's tracks were straight as an arrow. Frank's tracks meandered all over the field.

"Notice how your tracks wander aimlessly from the fence to the cattle to the woods and back again. And see how my tracks aim directly to my goal. There is an important lesson in that."

Years later as he reflected on that experience, Frank said, "I determined right then not to miss most things in life as my uncle had."

Imagination is the God-given power that energizes a weary brain. It enables us, as Len Sweet says, to get off the concrete of hard facts and logic so that we can wander around in the mud of creativity, fun, and laughter. Imagination refreshes the mind by helping us see the wonders in life, from the beauty and delicacy of a snowflake to the life-giving power of a drop of water to the innocent laugh of a little baby. After dealing with the pressures and demands of a long day, the imagination relaxes our mind by empowering us to have some fun—to climb a tree or walk barefoot in the grass or take a nap in the backyard. The gift of creativity—and we all have it—massages the mind back into health and vitality.

4. Repower the mind through God-given dreams. The imagination stimulates the mind by filling it with new dreams and ideas, dreams that add new energy and spark to what can become a dull routine. As that great scholar Batman (the Adam West version) once said, "What is a dream but a blueprint for courageous action."

After a long, body-punishing training run, it takes courage to run it again the next week. But after a nice, invigorating massage, the challenge no longer seems so daunting. After a long day at the office, it takes courage to get up and do it all over again the next day. A mind massaged by God-given dreams and ideas recharges the mental batteries and gives us the courage not only to head back to work, but also to head back to work with new insights that can transform the mission and ministry of the congregation.

So why not take a few moments right now and let God gently and tenderly massage the tired muscles in your mind? Feel the fingers of God's forgiveness knead out the sense of failure. Enjoy the fresh touch of God's healing love. Let your imagination run free. Let it give birth to a new dream for your life and ministry. Read a book or talk to a friend and let the insightful information work out the knots of old ideas and frustrated plans. Play with a child, or watch your favorite comedy. Let fun and laughter ease the mental stress and fatigue. It feels so-o-o good, doesn't it?

If you think that feels good, just wait until you experience the joy and power of a transformed, rejuvenated attitude.

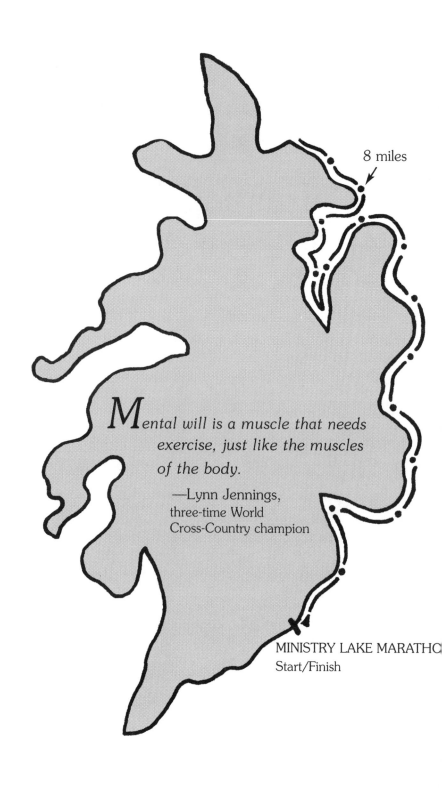

8 miles

*M*ental will is a muscle that needs
exercise, just like the muscles
of the body.

—Lynn Jennings,
three-time World
Cross-Country champion

MINISTRY LAKE MARATHON
Start/Finish

Training Tip #2
Adjust Your Attitude

I can do all things through him who strengthens me.
—Philippians 4:13 NRSV

Tom sat staring at the to-do list in front of him and shook his head. The Christmas show was just around the corner. How in the world did he ever imagine that he could handle the responsibility of putting a show like this together? He couldn't believe that "they" expected him to do all of this in the first place.

Glancing up at the month-to-month calendar hanging on his office wall, he could see that the Christmas show was only the beginning. After the show there would be multiple Christmas Eve services to plan, each of which, the pastor had informed him, had to be different from the next to attract different audiences. Right on the heels of Christmas would be the January Extravaganza, and soon Easter would be here with five more services to plan—each different from the others, of course. And the list went on and on. He knew at that moment that resigning would be the smartest thing he could do. But he also knew that the pastor wouldn't accept his resignation. He had been hired as the head of the music department because the church thought he was more than capable of handling the task.

He looked once again at his to-do list. Priority number one: fine-tune the budget for the Christmas season. Math had never been his best subject. He decided to skip number one and move on to number two. But the list seemed to grow before his eyes. It suddenly came alive, taunting him, daring him to tackle and conquer it. He needed to pick music, write a script, find musicians, audition actors, build sets, get the costumes, set the rehearsal schedule, and on and on it went. He could not possibly beat the beast before him. The list now had eyes and fangs. It stared at him like a menacing gargoyle.

His body decided to rebel and make its feelings known. First came the sweats. Beads of perspiration ran down his wrinkled forehead. His heart began to palpitate. It was as if the little drummer boy lived in his chest. The anxiety of being a failure weighed heavily on him.

He couldn't do it. The task was too great. Too much was expected of him. He could do only one thing. He rose from his chair, locked his office, and went home to take a long winter's nap. Maybe, if luck shined on him, he'd sleep right through Christmas. In any case, his to-do list could wait one more day.

While driving home, he found himself singing "I've got a new attitude," words from an old Patti LaBelle song. As his car slowly cruised into his driveway he wondered why that particular song would suddenly pop into his head. Oh well, it didn't matter. A nap was what he needed. A long nap.

In running a marathon, attitude is everything. As the race goes on and on the left part of the brain—the rational side—tries to tell you how crazy you are. It attempts to convince you that

Training Log: October 14.

Ran twenty-two miles today.
Took almost four hours.
Longest run of my life.
Hardest run of my life.
I don't think I can do this!

you can't do it. Running 26.2 miles doesn't make sense. It isn't logical. You have no business attempting such a run. In the early part of the run such thoughts don't have much of an impact. The excitement of the race carries you for awhile. But as the miles pile up, the doubts start wearing on you. The warm sun, the continuous pounding on the pavement, the growing blister, the kink in the hamstring—all challenge you to do the sensible thing and call it quits. And if you listen and give in to those doubts, you won't see the finish line no matter what kind of shape you're in.

The ministry marathon often challenges us with similar attitude-busting challenges: budget shortfalls, divided church councils, sick and/or dying members, sermon blocks, clergy jealousies, volunteers who don't show up, sixty hours of work and only fifty hours to do it in, and so on. We can probably handle them one by one. But when they start to pile up on us mile after mile, we find ourselves overwhelmed. The left part of the brain kicks in questioning our ability to get the job done. We experience debilitating discouragement and begin to doubt ourselves, our call, perhaps even God. Soon we lose hope. We no longer see the finish line, and even worse, we don't really care anymore.

The Power of Attitude

Jeff Galloway, Olympic marathoner and marathon guru, understands the energy-draining power of doubt, a power that blindsides all of us from time to time no matter what the endeavor. In his training sessions, he talks often about the antidote to doubt: a healthy attitude. He, along with other sports leaders, believes that while physical training is essential to running a strong race, attitude gets you over the finish line. So Galloway encourages runners to cultivate a healthy "belief environment"—an environment that stimulates the creative side of the brain with positive affirmations, optimism, and faith that will, in turn, counteract and diminish the power of doubt. This positive belief environment

- keeps the runner on automatic pilot, physically moving him or her forward even when the runner is doubting his or her capabilities.
- keeps positive motivation high even in the face of negative experiences.
- reaches down for motivation when it starts running low.
- monitors and conserves resources.
- intuitively stops and alerts the runner if he or she is under a health threat. (See Jeff Galloway, *Marathon* [Atlanta: Phidippides Publishing, 1996], pp. 21-23.)

Recent research further expands on the benefits of a healthy belief environment. It tells us that positive thinkers enjoy better overall health than pessimists do. Optimists, for example, respond to stress with smaller increases in blood pressure. They catch fewer infectious diseases. Their immune system works better. They age well and live longer on average than do those with a negative bent. In other words, a positive attitude is healthy for us.

So an important ingredient for running the marathon of ministry successfully is to cultivate a healthy belief environment. For an optimistic belief system keeps us in the race—and keeps us energized and healthy during the race—even when the circumstances suggest discouragement and defeat.

Cultivating an Attitude-Adjusting Environment

With that in mind, the following elements can help you build an attitude-adjusting environment that will keep you motivated throughout the whole race:

1. See yourself through the focused lens of Jesus Christ. A University of Michigan study discovered that the best predictor of general life satisfaction is not a great family life, lots of friends, or a healthy income, though these all help. Rather, the best predictor of happiness is satisfaction with oneself.

As ministry leaders, we often find it difficult to accept and appreciate ourselves. Some of us, for example, fearing pride or big-headedness, tend to dismiss our God-given gifts and talents. We find ourselves embarrassed at compliments and try to point people to Jesus rather than ourselves. Such God-pointing is good if it comes from a heart secure in its God-given worth and value. But such God-pointing can be a cover-up for false humility or a lack of worth and value. Too often failure, mistakes, and disappointment have led us to doubt ourselves, which is the prelude to race-breaking negative beliefs.

Loving and appreciating ourselves, on the other hand, leads to a positive, optimistic attitude. Self-appreciation sets us free from destructive, negative, can't-do thoughts and energizes us with the God-honoring belief that we can do all things through Christ.

When Pinocchio was first able to speak, he looked at his creator, Gepetto, and said, "I'm not sure who I am. But if I'm all right with you, then I guess I'm all right with me."

Ministry leaders often have self-doubts. But into those doubts comes Jesus with the good news that our Creator thinks we're all right. Jesus came to remind us that God believes in us. He tells us that God looks at us through the filtered lens of Jesus. That filter covers our failure and brokenness so that God sees us as forgiven. And as we see ourselves through that lens we find we can begin to believe in ourselves again—a belief that energizes us with an optimistic, ministry-empowering attitude.

2. Cultivate an attitude of optimism. The apostle Paul, in his letter to the Philippians, tells us that we can choose our attitude. And he encourages us to choose a faith-filled attitude by dwelling on those things that energize us with optimism. In other words, according to Paul, developing a healthy, optimistic, God-centered attitude is something we deliberately train to do by altering the way that we think.

Modern research affirms Paul's belief that we can learn to be optimistic people. We can choose to see the glass as half full or half empty. We can choose to interpret the latest ministry challenge as the end of the world or as a new chance to see God in action. As we fill our minds with positive, God-filled thoughts, we find that over time we cultivate a faith-filled response to life—a response that keeps us fresh for the marathon of ministry.

Arizona Senator John McCain credits optimism with helping him stay alive during five years in a North Vietnam prisoner of war camp. Two of those years were spent in solitary confinement. What kept him going, McCain says, was the fundamental belief that things in the end would be okay. That positive belief was not born out of some bubble-headed disregard of reality. Rather, McCain's optimism was rooted in his faith in God. He chose to see his situation from God's perspective—to view life from the perspective of the cross and Resurrection. He knew that when life is filled with crosses, faith says that God will have the final word—that the Resurrection is just around the corner. Thinking about and absorbing that promise cultivates in us energy-giving optimism.

3. Cultivate an attitude of hope. Perhaps the most pervasive attitude-drainer is hopelessness—the belief that nothing we do makes any difference. Martin Seligman, whose landmark research demonstrates our ability to choose optimism, calls this sense of hopelessness learned helplessness. Learned helplessness is the belief that, on the basis of past experience, there will always be an opposing force stronger than we are that will undo everything we do. In ministry that force may be the church council, power brokers, pioneers (those who built the church—or think they did!), or all of the above. Continuous battles with the disgruntled eats away at our will to go on.

God's cure for learned helplessness is hope—the assurance that the strongest force, barring none, is the power of the Resurrection.

In a large city in the United States, a local school system offers a program that sends teachers into hospitals to tutor children convalescing there for extended stays. One day a volunteer teacher was called upon to work with a young boy on his nouns and adverbs. The teacher had no idea why the student was in the hospital. Her first visit shocked her when she saw that the young boy was badly burned over most of his body. He was obviously in a great deal of pain. The teacher, deeply moved by his condition, had a hard time concentrating on the task at hand. When the hour was up, she left the room feeling like a total failure.

The next day she received a call from a hospital nurse who asked, "What did you do to that boy?" The teacher, assuming she'd done something terrible, began to apologize. But the nurse interrupted her and said, "No, no. You don't understand. We've been worried about that little guy. He didn't seem to have any will to live. But since your visit his whole attitude has changed. He's fighting back. He's decided to live."

Two weeks later the young boy explained the change. He admitted that he had given up hope until the teacher came to visit him. He said, "It suddenly hit me that they wouldn't send a teacher to work on nouns and adverbs with a dying boy, would they?"

Hope gave him a new lease on life. And it can give us a new lease on ministry.

4. Cultivate an attitude of praise. George Frideric Handel had reached the bottom. His right side was paralyzed. He was broke. His creditors threatened him with prison. He was so discouraged that he contemplated suicide. Instead, he chose to praise God—to focus on God's goodness rather than on his own desperate circumstances. Out of that experience came one of the greatest works of praise ever written—Handel's *Messiah* and the "Hallelujah Chorus."

An attitude of praise bursts through the tough, discouraging times of ministry by reminding us that God is good. And because God is good, ministry, at its core, is good even though for awhile it may seem challenging.

5. Cultivate a circle of cheerleaders. As my marathon drew closer, the doubts grew. I had already canceled two marathon attempts due to small, nagging injuries. Those injuries seemed to threaten my chances once again. Many days every part of my body hurt, including my hair. I wondered if I would ever run the race.

Thankfully, I had people pulling for me. Their faith and belief in me helped me believe in myself. For instance, my massage therapist continually talked about how great I would do during the marathon. As she worked out the knots and stiffness she prayed for me and thanked God in advance for the great run I would have. At times she was much more confident about my running and finishing the race than I was. My family offered me that same gift. They encouraged me to go for my dream, fully believing I would do it even when I wasn't sure.

Ministry is filled with naysayers. Church leaders often serve as lightning rods for disgruntled, disappointed, and hurting people. To survive and thrive in the ministry marathon, leaders need to surround themselves with positive cheerleaders, people who fill them with faith when doubts begin to creep in.

Choosing the Colors of Life

A physically challenged woman had a friend who approached her and said, "Affliction does so color life!" To which she responded, "It sure does. But I propose to choose the color." Adjusting our attitudes with a Jesus-oriented view of ourselves and with optimism, hope, praise, and a faith-inducing support system helps us choose positive, life-giving colors in ministry and life—colors that encourage us to keep running the race set before us with joy. And though we may grow weary, the God-centered belief that we can do all things through Christ will get us through.

I don't know about you, but all of this training talk is making me tired. It's time for a break!

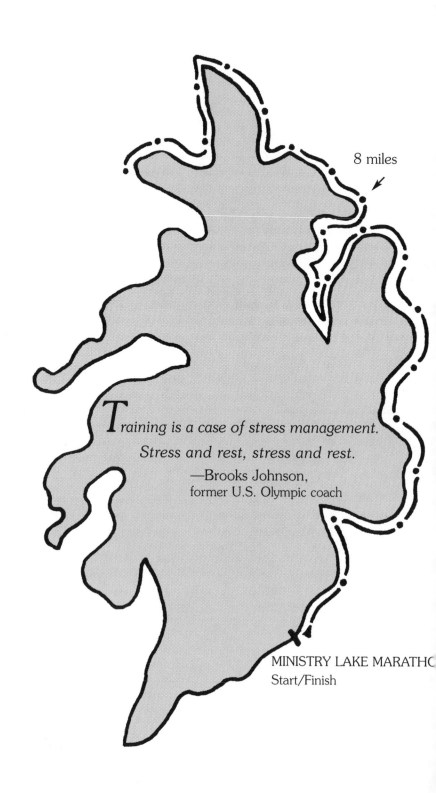

8 miles

Training is a case of stress management. Stress and rest, stress and rest.
—Brooks Johnson,
former U.S. Olympic coach

MINISTRY LAKE MARATHO
Start/Finish

Training Tip #3
Replenish Your Resources

Those who wait for the LORD shall renew their
strength, they shall mount up with wings like
eagles, they shall run and not be weary,
they shall walk and not faint.
—Isaiah 40:31 NRSV

*For the last five years Jason and Kathy worked side
by side in the missions department at their church.
They had known almost immediately when they met
fifteen years prior that God had an amazing plan for
the two of them. Two years after that meeting, they
married and their journey began.*

*They spent a few years in the mission field before start-
ing a family. But once children came along, they decided
to pursue ministry positions Stateside. They found themselves in Tennessee with the job of a lifetime. Along the
way, however, some things changed, and not necessarily
for the better.*

The pace had grown too fast. Not much downtime. Even finding an hour to grab lunch seemed almost impossible. Fast food was always the quickest and easiest solution to a set of growling stomachs. And drive-throughs made it even more convenient for them. They found they could grab a quick bite while enroute to their next meeting.

By the time they'd get home in the evening, after picking up their three kids at various after-school functions, dinner was usually a quick-fix of mac-n-cheese or frozen pizza. Occasionally a healthy TV dinner was thrown in for good measure. The kids needed their veggies after all.

Jason and Kathy did have a membership at the local health club, but they never used it. By the time dinner was done, homework completed, and chores finished, it was time to sit down and discuss the events for the following day. And, of course, monthly missions board meetings, occasional missions events, and missions fund-raisers dotted their calendars. Time simply didn't allow for trips to the club. Getting to bed often didn't happen until after midnight.

And soon the routine began to take its toll.

Jason had gained at least 40 pounds in the last five years. He felt sloppy and lethargic. His blood pressure had become a concern, as had his cholesterol level. The sparkle in his hazel eyes had dimmed to a flicker. And he had bags under his eyes that could carry groceries. Kathy often kidded him that the red lines running through the whites of his eyes looked like a road map to his brain.

As for Kathy, she began to notice that she could no longer remove her wedding ring when she washed her hands. But that wasn't nearly as bad as the realization that she didn't quite fit into her office chair as well as she used to. Occasionally she noticed a shortness of breath when she climbed a flight of stairs. And, like Jason, she felt tired all the time.

The mission field had been much different. Jason and Kathy had purposefully set aside time to walk every day and get some fresh air. The food in the country where they served was usually healthy and delicious. They missed those days. The cultural lifestyle was more laid-back and easygoing. Although they had jobs and responsibilities, the unrealistic expectations they felt in the States didn't seem to exist in the field. Now the pace was simply out of control. They had no time to care for themselves. The ministry consumed too much of their lives. In the back of their minds they knew that if their bodies began to fall apart, their ministry would suffer as well. But they were too busy to worry about that. So they pushed those thoughts away and went on with the business at hand.

Finally, something happened that forced them to review their priorities. They were asked to participate in a friendly game of basketball in order to raise money for the upcoming missions trip. The first five minutes of the game were a breeze for both Jason and Kathy. But from that point on, everything went downhill. Jason could barely dribble the ball from one end of the court to the other. He found himself gasping for air. He could hear his friends yelling from the sidelines, "Hey, Jason! Do you need oxygen? You could use your belly as the basketball!" And while he played along with the humor, it hit a bit too close to home.

Kathy, too, struggled to keep up. After several minutes, she called a time-out and benched herself. She told herself that her motive was to enable others to get into the game, but she knew better. The truth was that she couldn't breathe.

On the way home they sat silently wondering how they

had gotten to this point. Finally, Kathy spoke up and put words to their thoughts. "We need to fix this, Jason. Our bodies are all messed up. We don't get enough sleep. I don't fit in my desk chair anymore. I'm so tired all the time that it's affecting my excitement for ministry." Kathy had a way of getting right to the heart of the matter.

"Well," said Jason, "what should we do?"

"I'm not sure. Let's stop at the ice-cream shop and discuss it over a banana split."

"Okay. And then we'll start our diet and exercise program on Monday."

"And we'll get some sleep, too. Yep. Monday it is."

As they drove into the parking lot of the ice-cream shop they both knew they would have this discussion again. If not next Monday, then maybe the Monday after that. There just wasn't the time to take care of themselves, not right now anyway. Maybe when things calmed down a bit. Maybe then they would do something about it. But not today.

> **Training Log: December 2.**
> Excellent run.
> The two days' rest really helped.
> Best run in the last three weeks.
> I feel great.

According to a recent Louis Harris poll, 86 percent of us claim to be chronically stressed. One out of 4 of us say that we're stressed to the point of exhaustion. Thirty-eight percent of us always feel rushed. The American Academy of Family Physicians estimates that 60 percent of the problems brought to a physician are stress-related. Of the top twenty prescription drugs, eleven of them treat stress disorders. Thirteen billion doses of tranquilizers, barbiturates, and amphetamines are prescribed each year. The cost of work time missed due to stress and its related illnesses is over $200 billion annually. No wonder stress is considered the disease of this century!

Those numbers, however, represent more than simply statistics. Those of us in ministry know personally the challenges of stress and the toll it can take on our lives. Stress can leave us drained mentally, emotionally, physically, and spiritually. If we're not careful, it can rob us of our energy midway through the race, leaving us burned-out and seriously considering a career change.

Perhaps this describes you: You know you're stressed and tired when

- you feel like the morning after, but you haven't been anywhere.
- you get winded playing chess.
- your mind makes contracts your body can't meet.
- you look forward to a dull evening at home.
- a fortune-teller offers to read your face.

Bottom line: If you're in ministry, you're going to experience more than your fair share of energy-draining stress.

An Energy-Replenishing Plan

God created us to live life and do ministry with energy and vitality. And with proper training and healthy doses of rest, we can replenish our resources and keep ourselves in the race. Below are three keys that can help you increase your energy level.

1. Expend energy to receive energy. In the play *Hamlet,* William Shakespeare writes:

What a piece of work is man! how noble in reason! how infinite in faculties! in form and moving how express and admirable! in action how like an angel! in apprehension how like a god! the beauty of the world! the paragon of animals!

The psalmist puts it this way: "You are the one who put me together inside my mother's body, and I praise you because of the wonderful way you created me. Everything you do is marvelous! Of this I have no doubt" (Psalm 139:13-14 CEV).

The human body is remarkable! For example, it's made up of over 100 trillion cells. It houses a little muscle we call the heart, which weighs between 8 and 12 ounces and beats on average seventy-two times per minute, with a four-tenth second rest between beats. And it does this minute after minute, day after day, for an average of over seventy years. The heart pumps 4 quarts of blood through the body every minute. That adds up to 2H billion heartbeats pumping 35 million gallons of blood throughout the average life.

The body also includes a 3-pound brain, which thinks, reacts, feels, dreams, and enables us to move—a gift 500 million times more complex than the world's most complicated computer. And built into our bodies is an amazing ability to survive—an immune system that science cannot come close to copying. God has created us with the incredible ability to fight off disease and heal quickly.

The body is an amazing creation. But for the body to run at peak performance—in order for the body to energize itself—it needs to expend energy. Unfortunately, we don't live in a society that makes it easy to keep our bodies finely tuned. We've moved from a labor-intensive society in which we worked with our bodies to an information age in which we work with our minds. Ministry in particular is a job that has a high demand for sitting.

The result is a nation that is out of shape. A recent survey of Americans found that three-fourths of us are overweight. One-fourth of us are actually obese. One fitness expert says that ministers are the most out-of-shape professionals in the country. And a tired body leads to a tired, de-energized ministry.

God places a high value on our bodies and put a lot of thought, creativity, and energy into designing and creating them. Caring for them not only honors God but also gives us the energy we need to stay in the marathon of ministry. In fact, taking care of our bodies is a spiritual issue, as important to our well-being as caring for our souls.

So here it is—the key to reenergizing our bodies: exercise. God created our bodies for movement. When we expend energy, we receive energy. And in ministry, we have to schedule time for exercise—to move our bodies and exercise our hearts.

The benefits of exercise are amazing. Exercise

- makes you smarter.
- converts fat to energy.
- keeps you young longer.
- can cut the risk of heart disease by almost 50 percent.
- can help you live longer and better.
- helps you sleep better.
- helps you better cope with problems.
- reduces stress. (Note: Twenty-two percent of those who exercise feel rushed compared to 44 percent of those who don't exercise.)

Starting an exercise program, be it walking, running, swimming, or using one of a host of cardiovascular machines, is one of the most energizing gifts you can give yourself. We all know we should exercise. But if you value yourself enough to do it (after checking first with your doctor), it will keep you in the ministry marathon for life.

2. Fuel up. In training for my marathon I had to learn how to fuel up while running. Drinking a sports drink, ingesting an energy gel, or eating a piece of power bar every mile or so gave me the energy I needed for the next mile. Several minutes after fueling up I could feel the drink or gel working its magic. In addition to that, I needed to watch my daily diet and eat the kinds of food that would quickly replenish my resources and keep me in shape for training and the race itself.

When it comes to diet, Jack Lalane asks, "Would you get your dog up in the morning and give him a cup of coffee, a cigarette, and a doughnut? Of course not! You'd kill the dog."

God created our bodies in such a way that when they receive the right kind of fuel, they will run at peak performance. Sadly, the right kind of fuel in today's world seems to be equated with boring and unappetizing. Who really wants to eat salads every day when you can have a hamburger? Who wants an apple when you can have ice cream?

Perhaps these tongue-in-cheek diet hints can help as you think through fueling up:

- If no one sees you eat it, it has no calories.
- If you drink a sugar-free can of pop along with a candy bar, they cancel each other out.
- When eating with someone else, calories don't count if you both eat the same thing.
- Foods used for medicinal purposes never count, such as hot chocolate, toast, and cheesecake.
- If you fatten up everyone else around you, you look thinner.

• Movie-related foods, such as Milk Duds, popcorn with butter, and candy-coated almonds, don't count because they are simply a part of the entertainment experience and not a part of one's personal fuel.

The truth is, we are what we eat. If we put leaded gas in an unleaded car, we will destroy the car. The same is true for our bodies. They need the right kind of fuel. And as we learn to eat right, we'll discover a new energy for life and ministry.

3. Rest up. Back in my late twenties, when I first dreamed of running a marathon, I looked at training programs that emphasized putting in heavy-duty mileage. Many plans emphasized running every day with a long run once a week. Each week could add up to hundreds of miles. My back injury never gave me the chance to train under one of those plans.

When I decided to train for a marathon several years later, I discovered a new philosophy toward marathoning developed by Jeff Galloway. That philosophy included low mileage and *ample rest*. In training thousands of marathoners like me—people interested in finishing, not competing—Galloway discovered the remarkable power of rest and the replenishing of one's resources. In a very real sense, rest became as crucial to the success of the marathon as did putting in the miles. Rest replaces the stress of training with new energy and vitality, making the running of the marathon an enjoyable experience.

Those who train wisely for that 26.2-mile race do so by taking rest seriously. Every three to four weeks they cut back on their mileage for a few days. Two to three weeks before the race itself they "taper" down their miles. You'd think that you'd want to put in as many miles as possible the closer you get to the race, but the opposite is true. As race day draws near you want to rest by cutting back on miles.

Galloway also recommends this innovation in marathoning: Walk a minute every mile. He has learned through experience that walking a minute every mile rests the leg muscles and can actually help a person run faster than if he or she doesn't walk. Rest is the key to replenishing our resources for the marathon of ministry.

Over the last couple of years, articles have been written on how sleep-deprived we are. Long meetings, counseling sessions, last-minute sermon preparation, anxiety over making budget, filling in for no-show volunteers, and so on can rob us of sleep. And without the right amount of sleep we start becoming ineffective. Busy schedules keep us at work even on our day off. And many of us don't have the time or resources to take our vacations. Envisioning the pile of work on our desks when we get back robs us of the desire to leave.

Wise ministry marathoners learn the art of leisure. The word *leisure* comes from a Latin word meaning "to be permitted." Those who thrive in the marathon of ministry permit themselves time to rest. They make it a point to get the right amount of sleep. They take their days off. They use up all their vacation time on vacations. Throughout the day they take a mental or literal walking break. They find a hobby that helps replenish sagging resources. One psychologist insists that if people could learn to relax and quiet their bodies, they could cut the chance of catching a cold and other respiratory illnesses in half.

Jesus continually took time out to rest up. With no cars around, he was in great physical shape because he walked everywhere. But he also knew the importance of getting away to rest a while. And if Jesus needed to rest, we certainly need to as well.

Caring for yourself physically is a spiritual issue. And as you take the necessary steps to replenish your resources you will find an enhanced sense of worth and value, new vitality and enthusiasm for ministry, and the energy to help you stay in the ministry marathon. On top of that, it just plain feels good to be healthy and in shape.

So put on your walking shoes and head outside for a nice, refreshing walk. Maybe you'll want to call someone you care about and have them join you.

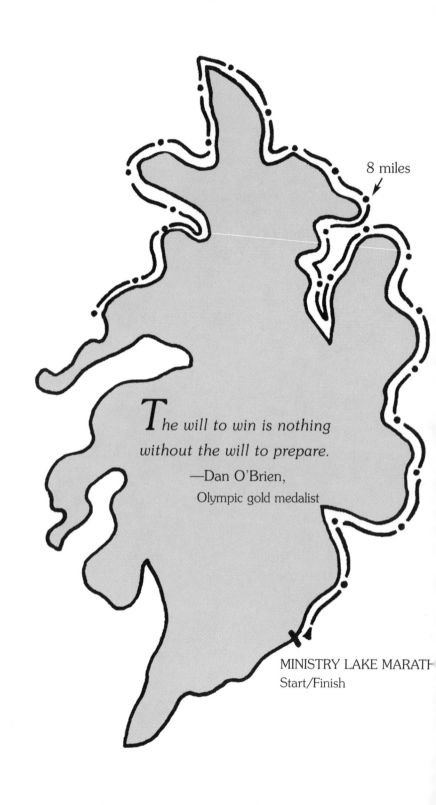

8 miles

*T*he will to win is nothing
without the will to prepare.
—Dan O'Brien,
Olympic gold medalist

MINISTRY LAKE MARATH
Start/Finish

Training Tip #4
Affirm Your Affections

A friend is always a friend,
and relatives are born to share our troubles.
—Proverbs 17:17 CEV

Another beautiful spring day. Looking out his office window, he gazed longingly at the blossoming trees and flowering plants bordering the brick building that seemed to consume more of his life than did his own home. His eyes focused on a small bird sitting in the tree waiting eagerly for the return of its mother and the scrumptious feast she'd be carrying in her beak. The total dependence of that little bird on its parent overwhelmed him with a sense of loss. And then, as if it could tell where his thoughts were going, the phone interrupted his brief moment of introspection.

"Hello. This is Dr. Davis. Can I help you?" He'd received his doctorate in marriage and family counseling four years prior. Since then, his job at a large mid-

western church had kept him busier than he ever could have imagined. "Yes, Mrs. Johnson. How can I help?"

"Doctor, it's my son again. Things are going from bad to worse."

The call took twenty minutes, during which time Dr. Davis agreed to see Mrs. Johnson's wayward son later that afternoon. After hanging up the phone, he glanced at his day-planner and discovered that he had just made a dreadful scheduling error. His son was playing in a championship soccer tournament at precisely the time that he had agreed to meet with Mrs. Johnson's son. He doubted that his son would understand his missing another game. He had missed four games already, and missing this one would surely cause problems not just with his son but also with his wife, Betsy. Oh well, he thought, they would just have to understand. Yeah. Right.

He decided to put off the dreaded phone call to his wife for a bit while he checked his schedule for the rest of the day. As usual, he had scheduled counseling sessions one after another from morning until dinner. He'd have to make the call home during his ten-minute lunch break.

The morning blew by without much trouble. Noon came and went, and all thoughts of his son's game or his wife's righteous indignation flew from his mind. His meeting with Mrs. Johnson and her son was tense but went as well as could be expected. It seemed the son had some deep-seated anger toward his father, who made lots of promises but seldom followed through. Dr. Davis suggested a session with the father and son and then separate sessions for each as well. The son's final remark on his way out the door caught Dr. Davis's attention:

"I wonder if he'll make more time for you, Doc, than he does for me?"

Suddenly a soccer game flashed through Dr. Davis's

mind. He knew then that he would pay when he got home. But worse yet, he knew that he deserved everything he got. He was no better than the father of the boy he had just counseled. He felt a bit hypocritical, to say the least.

How had his life got to this point? How did the Mrs. Johnsons of the world become more important than spending time with his own family? When was the last time he took his wife out for dinner or spent an afternoon with his son or shared some time over a soda with his best friend, Mike?

He realized how much he had missed sharing with Mike the highs and lows of his life. He longed for the romance and togetherness that used to be second nature in his marriage. And just once he'd like for his son to ask his advice the way he did when his son was younger. Dr. Davis's thoughts strayed to a small boy with blond curly hair who had somehow, overnight, turned into a young man.

The doctor sat back down at his desk and stared out the window. The bright sunlight had been replaced by the glow of the moon. And as he looked out he could see the mother bird sitting in her nest gathering her young chicks under her wings. "That's how it's supposed to be," he spoke out loud. "But how do I get it back?" And in his heart a small voice whispered, "Start with a hug and an apology, and move forward from there." And that's what he did.

> **Training Log**: September 4.
>
> Ran the canals with Dave and Staci.
> Nice to have the company.
> The run seemed to go better and faster.

When I prepared for my first marathon, I did most of my

training alone. I ran for hours and hours by myself and actually looked forward to the alone time. It gave me a chance to pray, unwind, dream, and "get away" from the noise. Wired as an introvert, I thoroughly enjoy running by myself.

I ran the marathon, however, with my brothers Jeff and Dave. From the moment we started the run we joked, we talked, we encouraged each other, we checked in to see how one another was doing. When Jeff's knee began to give him problems, Dave ran ahead to alert the medical team while I ran with Jeff, trying to keep him going. Their camaraderie made the run an exceptional, rewarding experience.

Several months later I decided (after promising myself otherwise) to train for a second marathon. I wanted to prove to myself that the first race wasn't a fluke. Jeff agreed to run with me again, but about a month before the event, he had to pull out. So I was on my own.

I headed to the race alone. I stood around—by myself—in the dark early hours of the morning trying to stay loose and warm before the run was to begin. I eventually made my way to the starting line. I stood there with hundreds of other runners, but I was virtually alone. I didn't know anyone. For the most part I ran in silence. I still enjoyed the experience because I need and like my alone time. I even knocked five minutes off my Walt Disney World time. But I learned that running with others—particularly during a significant event—adds an energy and power that running by oneself cannot give.

The point is to find the balance between those times when ministry calls us to be alone and when we need to plug in to the gift of others, taking advantage of the support and encouragement they offer.

The Challenge of Ministry Relationships

Healthy relationships with family and friends provide the stability, security, and support necessary for the long, often-draining ministry run. They give our lives balance, love, and refuge—essential ingredients for health and well-being in ministry.

The natural tug of ministry, however, often pulls us away from relationships. Ministry, by its very essence, can leave us feeling isolated and lonely. For example, it calls for a high level of confidentiality. That confidentiality can burden pastors, staff, and even certain volunteers without providing them an outlet for dealing with it. They must carry the information alone, with no way to process it. In addition to that, ministry encourages long hours, usually evenings, that take us away from our families.

Because of the nature of ministry, many ministry people find it difficult to develop close friendships with parishioners. Perhaps others in the congregation will get jealous. Maybe the parishioner, because of the close relationship with the ministry person, will have a hard time receiving ministry from him or her. Or, maybe the parishioner will, for whatever reason, share some personal things with other members that the ministry person shared in confidence. Ministry is tough on supportive relationships, but without them we run out of steam and could risk dropping out of the race.

Building Healthy Family Relationships

As I prepared for ordination several pastors shared with me an important piece of advice. I could tell that they wished they had been given (or had heeded) such advice at the beginning of their careers. The advice went something like this: Don't ignore those most important to you; make your family your top priority. Many who shared that insight with me did so out of their own personal pain. They had neglected their families in order to build great ministries. In the process, they lost those they loved and cared for the most.

Building strong relationships, like everything else about the marathon of ministry, takes some training, wisdom, and discipline. For great relationships happen when we make them a priority and do the things that keep them healthy. With that in mind, the following thoughts can help us reaffirm and strengthen the significant relationships in our lives.

1. Tips for a healthy marriage. Do you remember the day when your dad or someone else significant in your life placed your hand on your husband-to-be's hand? Do you remember standing in the front of the church and watching your bride walk down the aisle toward you? Do you remember the hopes and dreams you had as you stood before your family and friends to be joined as husband and wife? Has ministry enhanced those dreams or crushed them? Has it helped you grow close together, or has the busyness of the call robbed you of time and intimacy together? In the leadership conferences sponsored by my church we often hear church leaders, and particularly their spouses, pour out deep-seated hurt and even anger over the toll ministry has taken on their marriages. None of us go into ministry expecting it to damage our marriages. Unfortunately it happens all too often.

While it goes beyond the scope of this book to offer detailed help for derailed marriages, the following few training components can help put the zip and excitement back into marriage:

- **Prayer**. Catholic sociologist Andrew Greeley says that couples who pray together are twice as likely to describe their marriage as being in the falling-in-love stage as those who don't pray together. They also have a higher level of satisfaction in the more intimate areas of marriage. He even goes so far as to describe their love as "ecstasy." Now that should get you praying together again!

- **Affection.** A college security officer was making the rounds in the parking lot about midnight after registration day. He noticed—through the steamy windows of one car—a couple holding each other as couples sometimes do. He tapped on the window. To his surprise a middle-aged man rolled down the window and, obviously embarrassed, said, "We're sorry, officer, but we just left our youngest son, our baby, over there in the dorm. It's the first time his mother and I have been alone in twenty-seven years."

  Healthy marriages set aside time for demonstrations of love. Couples get into the habit of looking for "affection moments." Hugging, phone calls, flowers, date nights (every week), and e-mails help to ensure that the marriage thrives in the midst of a busy ministry.

- **Time away.** Ministry is a twenty-four-hour-a-day career. Most of us find it impossible to leave it completely behind when we close the door to the office. In order to fully concentrate on their marriage, healthy couples take time away from the office—and that usually means time away from home. Well-timed two-to-four-day getaways three or four times a year can go a long way toward refilling the marriage tank.

- **Ogling.** To ogle means to glance with an amorous invitation. Perhaps one of the reasons why ministry marriages grow stale is that we stop flirting with our spouses. Some good ogling every day can spice up a marriage and in the process reenergize us for the ministry marathon.

2. Tips for staying in touch with your children.
When I was in junior high, the local pastor's kid attended my school. He was always getting into trouble. I couldn't understand what his problem was. His parents seemed to be very nice people. The church was dynamic and well known throughout the community. But apparently he had a hard time adjusting to life as a P.K. (pastor's kid). I later learned that P.K.s have a reputation for often being troubled.

When I became a parent, I made a promise to myself that I would do whatever I could to protect my children from the pressure of being P.K.s. I thought that the large size of our congregation might help, since the kids would be fairly anonymous. Because our church is so contemporary and "non-churchy," I hoped that perhaps the usual pressures of having to live up to certain standards and expectations wouldn't apply here. And we simply didn't make a big deal out of being a ministry family.

So I was quite surprised some years ago when my daughter, who was ten years old at the time, vented some of her anger at being a P.K. She talked about how her friends teased her. She shared the hurt she experienced when her friends' parents would rip into the church in front of her. She related how it disappointed her that church people seemed to be as "human" as other people.

Just the other day, completely unsolicited, my fifteen-year-old son talked about the pressure he felt by being my son. He said he sensed that people expected him to act a certain way. Making matters worse, he felt that if he didn't conform to those expectations, people would think less of me or the church.

I had the chance to assure him that I was proud of him just as he is—that I like his unique style and personality. It was an eye-opening, and yet wonderful, conversation for both of us. I thank God my kids have actually coped pretty well with a pressure I never knew as a kid.

Ministry kids do have it tough. After all, their parents work for God. Or, their parents make volunteering some of their time to God a priority. So if they get mad at their parents for choosing a ministry career or because the church keeps their parents too busy, the kids feel like they're actually getting mad at God. That's pressure! In response, we need to make sure that we do what we can to make our children the priority in our lives. Below are a few training essentials for helping our kids with the dreaded P.K. or M.K. (ministry kid) syndrome.

- **Time.** A dad was visiting his son's class one day and overheard him talking with three of his friends. One of the friends bragged, "My daddy is a doctor and he makes lots of money and we have a swimming pool." The second friend said, "Oh yeah! My daddy is a lawyer and he flies to Washington and talks to the president." The third boy, not to be outdone, said, "Well, my daddy owns a company and we have our own airplane." The dad was curious as to how his son would respond and was delighted when he said, "Well, my daddy is here."

  As John Drescher said in a Father's Day message:

  Now is the time to love. Tomorrow the baby won't be rocked, the toddler won't be asking, "Why?" The schoolboy won't need help with his lessons, nor will he bring his school friends home for some fun. Tomorrow the teenager will have made her major decisions. (Larry Christenson, *The Christian Family* [Minneapolis: Bethany House, 1970])

  Family fun nights, special dates with our kids, surprise outings, and so on demonstrate love and warmth to our children and keep the lines of communication open. For kids, quality time equals quantity time. And in the midst of the hectic ministry marathon, making time for our children is essential.

- **Compliments.** A little girl had been particularly naughty one day. So, during family prayer time, her dad recited the list of bad things she had done. Later Mom found her little girl crying in her bedroom. When she asked what was wrong, the little girl said, "Daddy always tells God the bad things about me. He never tells the good things I do."

    Great parents learn how to attach honor and value to their kids. Instead of focusing on their children's faults, they continually celebrate their children's strengths. They give praise and compliments freely and often. They shower their children with worth and a healthy sense of God-given dignity.

- **A listening ear.** On my journey to ministry I attended four years of college and four years of seminary. I studied Greek and Hebrew. I read the great philosophers and dug into the greatest theological minds of the day. Plus, I have forty years of life experience. So when my kids come to me for help, I'm armed and ready to pontificate for hours—to enlighten their wondering minds through the use of my vast wisdom. How humbling it is to hear from them that what they want from me is not another sermon, but an open, sympathetic, listening ear. That's a tough one for someone whose career is built on talking. But that listening ear is one of the greatest gifts I can give my kids.

- **Demonstrations of love.** A recent study suggests that because of the increased social, financial, and personal demands we all face, hugging happens 20 percent less today than it did ten years ago. Yet hugging and meaningful touch is vitally important to our overall health and well-being. Jesus often used touch to demonstrate love. For example, he reached out his hands and blessed the children. Hugs, pats on the back, kisses, and other forms of healthy touch express volumes of love to our kids, keep us on the same page, and impart a strong sense of self-esteem to them.

- **Faith.** A young boy was busy drawing a picture. His mom watched him for several minutes and then asked what he was doing. "Drawing a picture of God." Mom smiled and said, "Well, honey, you can't do that. Nobody knows what God looks like." The young artist put down his pencil, admired his picture, and said, "They will in a moment."

Sometimes, in an attempt to shelter our kids from too much religiosity, ministry people will downplay faith nurturing in their kids. Not wanting to turn them off to faith, we can run the risk of not offering a faith life to our children at all. But children need a picture of what God looks like. They long for an authentic, personal experience of God. As parents, we can model faith for them even though faith is our "job" or heavy volunteer commitment. Reading Bible stories to our kids, praying with them, finding a place to worship with them (if for some reason they can't worship with you at your church), and listening to their doubts and struggles—without judging—can help plant seeds of faith that will blossom and grow as our kids move into adulthood.

3. Tips for developing a network of supportive friends. Finding a close friend while in ministry can be tough. We have to be careful who we trust. We need to surround ourselves with people who can maintain confidentiality, who can pray with us and for us without being intimidated, who can laugh at our mistakes, correct us when needed, and support us no matter what. Ministry people need someone with whom they can be vulnerable. For many, their spouses meet that need. Others turn to friends, sometimes because they don't have a spouse or because they don't want to burden their spouse with ministry stuff.

Some ministry people have found wonderful friendships with like-minded people in other congregations: Senior pastors meeting with other senior pastors (even cross-denominationally), music directors meeting with other music directors, volunteer Sunday school directors meeting with other volunteer leaders, and so on. Some leaders "pray up" a small group of highly dependable, trustworthy people from within the congregation who become their accountability and support team. With the advent of the Internet, many ministry leaders are finding new ways to connect with their "support team" across the country and around the world. Even Jesus needed a group of friends.

The Power of Cheerleaders

After over four and a half hours of running through Walt Disney World, I heard a familiar voice shouting "Dad!" I looked up and saw my son, Mike, jumping to the front of the crowd and waving. I asked him where Mom and Alycia were standing. He pointed up ahead, and soon I saw several faces I recognized—friends and family members cheering us on. After I crossed the finish line, they ran over to hug me, to "ooooh and aaaaah" over my finisher's medal, and to tell me how proud they were of me. Having them there at the end of the race to share in my "big accomplishment" was the highlight of the marathon.

My second marathon, as I mentioned, was a different story. After running for four hours, fifty minutes, and thirty-nine seconds, I crossed the finish line. I handed in my race tab, put on my medal, and stood there—alone. I had just finished a huge race and I had no one to share it with me. I looked around as people hugged family and friends. While I felt good about what I had just done, I also felt somewhat empty inside. So, after hanging out for fifteen minutes, I hopped into the car and headed back to the hotel. The end of my hard work and training seemed somewhat anticlimactic.

I learned a significant lesson that day: Success (and failure, for that matter) is meant to be shared. While personal achievements fill us with excitement and joy, that excitement and joy takes on new energy and power when others enjoy it with us. In fact, success can actually be somewhat hollow without someone else to taste it with us. And failure can be down right devastating when faced alone.

Healthy relationships keep us charged, healthy, balanced, and focused during the marathon of ministry. Trusted friends and family members cheer us on when we win, lift us up when we fall, and love us no matter what. And best of all, they remind us that we're not alone. Taking time alone is important. Surrounding ourselves with supportive relationships, however, is absolutely essential.

But where in the world do we find the time to do ministry, spend time with family and friends, take alone time, and care for ourselves? A day is only so long!

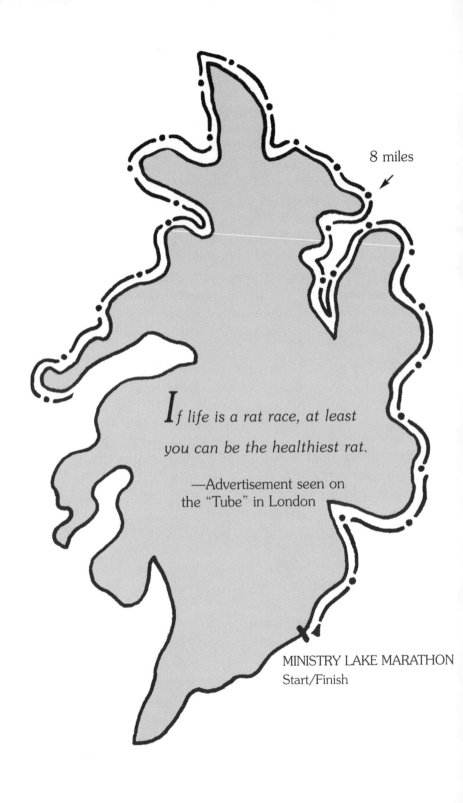

8 miles

If life is a rat race, at least you can be the healthiest rat.

—Advertisement seen on the "Tube" in London

MINISTRY LAKE MARATHON
Start/Finish

Training Tip #5
Track Your Time

Teach us to use wisely all the time we have.

—Psalm 90:12 CEV

The phone rang again. So far her calendar was full for the next three weeks. She knew who was on the other end of the line without picking up the receiver, and her stomach started tying itself up like a pretzel. She looked over at her husband, who sat at the table calmly drinking coffee, imploring him with her eyes to please take the call for her. His eyes responded, "No way, honey. You gotta do this on your own."

She picked up the phone and slowly raised it, but before the receiver touched her ear she could hear the voice she had come to dread: Mary Lou Finkelman, children's ministries coordinator and quick-talker extraordinaire.

"Hi, Jan. Did I wake you? I hope not. I know it's Saturday and I won't keep you long but as you know the

annual fall festival fund-raiser is coming up and you know how everyone loves your decorations and we thought of doing something new this year where instead of all the normal pumpkins and hay bales we thought we'd go more along the lines of a theme carnival you know like Mardi Gras or something like that but we decided to let you choose the theme and as long as you are doing the decorations I thought you could plan the food, too . . ."

The woman never stopped. Jan and her husband, Kirk, had already discussed the fall festival and Jan's need to say no. But Jan knew the committee would need her help. And Mary Lou Finkelman was so pushy!

As Jan stood listening to Mary Lou Finkelman ramble on and on, the pretzel in her stomach became tighter and tighter. She couldn't get a word in edgewise.

Kirk sat at the table, a small grin playing across his mouth and a slight tremor of a giggle beginning to erupt from his belly. He had to leave the room before he laughed out loud. Jan would surely throttle him otherwise.

Jan felt abandoned by Kirk as he left the room, but she knew he found this situation hilarious. He had told her over and over to cut back on her volunteer work. But she had the hardest time saying no to people in need. Her problem, as he always said, was that she had too big a heart, if that's possible.

"So, Jan, will you do the decorations and food planning for us this year?"

"Well, I," and that's as far as she got before Mary Lou Finkelman screamed in delight. "Oh, good, Jan! We knew we could count on you." And with that parting remark, Jan added another date to her already overcrowded calendar. And as she sighed, the phone began ringing again and Jan's stomach knot tightened further.

George Villa, an Evangelical Lutheran Church in America pastor, has done a profile on two groups of pastors: those in declining churches and those leading growing congrega-

Training Log: March 18.

Not sure how long I ran today. I forgot to start my watch. Frustrating, because I think I was running at a faster pace than normal.

tions. The study offers some interesting insights:

Pastors in declining congregations

- feel overwhelmed by "the job."
- have too much paper work, taking up 45 to 55 percent of the weekly hours.
- work longer hours (sixty to eighty per week).
- spend less quality and quantity time with their families.
- have almost no time for personal prayer and devotions.
- find their attention focused on crisis resolution and conflict.
- experience high levels of burnout.

Pastors in growing congregations

- manage "the job."
- spend less time on paper work (20 to 25 percent of the weekly hours).
- tend to work fewer hours (fifty to fifty-five per week).
- spend more quality and quantity time with their families.
- spend about 1½ hours in personal prayer and devotions.
- focus their attention on faith and spiritual develop-ment—of themselves and their congregation.
- experience a high level of excitement about their ministry.

The major difference between the two profiles? Those who fit the first profile find themselves managed by their schedules. Those in the second profile have learned the art of tracking their time.

Only So Many Hours in a Day!

Stephanie is a forty-two-year-old business administrator and mother of three. Unfortunately, her job increasingly takes up more and more of her time. As a result, she had to cancel several after-school events with her oldest daughter. Her daughter, not surprisingly, didn't handle it well. At one point she lashed out at her mother and said, "You care more about your work than you care about me." Stephanie does try hard to keep things in balance. But the demands of life seem to be taking control. In meeting with her counselor she said, "Life in the fast lane is getting to me. I've lost complete control of my life."

Most of us know exactly how Stephanie feels. The demands of life can overwhelm us. Especially in ministry. Ministry doesn't take time off. Emergencies don't honor a 9-to-5 schedule. Budgets don't always allow for much needed help. Many of us in ministry, whether we're paid staff or nonpaid staff, increasingly have to deal with a seemingly shrinking amount of time. Eventually life wrestles itself from our control and begins to manage us, leaving us too few hours to get everything done.

Yet God wisely created each day to last twenty-four hours. When maximized to their fullest, those twenty-four hours offer us plenty of time to do all that God calls us to do. The key is to use that time effectively each day. That's obvious. What's not so obvious is how to do it practically every day.

Chasing the Urgent or Enjoying the Important

All kinds of books have been written to help us better manage our time. But when all is said and done, tracking our time boils down to the ability to differentiate between the urgent and the important. And in ministry that's not always easy, for the two can often look alike.

The urgent demands that something be done right now. It never respects commitments or time. It doesn't care about what really matters in life. It wants its way right now. And often the urgent isn't all that important.

The important, on the other hand, takes the long look. It begins with the big picture. It seeks to use one's time according to what will have the greatest impact long term, and in the process, finds the power and courage to say no and yes when appropriate. The urgent punches the clock. The important uses a compass. By learning to track our time by the compass rather than the clock, we'll be better prepared to weave our way through the urgent so we can get to the important. The following "tracking points" can help us make better use of the compass.

1. Track your purpose. What is it God has called you to do? What is your purpose in life? In ministry? What gifts and talents has God given you that might provide insights into your purpose? Are you gifted in counseling but spend too much time in administration? Are you wired to preach but find little time to hone that skill because of too many hospital calls? Do you have a knack for developing the faith life of people but have little time to do it because you have so many meetings to run? What aspects of ministry set your heart singing? What parts drain you of energy? Gaining insight into your God-given purpose will help you better manage your time. The pastors in the growing-church profile have done that. They know their purpose. They then recruit and train others (both paid and nonpaid) to fill in their "gaps."

2. Track your priorities. While I was in Germany sharing this material with a group of Christian leaders, a man asked, "I work full time as a pastor. I also have a family to care for. On top of that, I have a house and yard to keep up, and so on. How do I find the time to do all of that, plus everything you're talking about in the area of self-care?"

I replied that it boiled down to priorities. For example, my priority is to keep myself healthy for my family and my ministry. That's more important to me than yard work. In fact, I hate yard work. So I hire someone to do it for me. The expense for hiring a crew versus my time to do the yard myself makes it worth it for me. In other words, getting our priorities straight helps us better manage our time.

What do you value in life? What is most important to you? Family? Career? Volunteering? God? Into what order do those priorities fall? Does the way you spend your time reflect those priorities and their scale of importance?

Along with determining our overarching life values, we must also build the habit of prioritizing the day-to-day matters of ministry. Otherwise the minutia of life will consume us and the urgent will begin to take over.

The Bethlehem Steel Corporation was struggling, so its president, Charles Schwab, hired consultant Ivy Lee to help out. Schwab agreed to pay Lee anything within reason if Lee's suggestion helped the company. A few days later Lee submitted his plan. He suggested that Schwab, before leaving the office at night, write down the most important tasks that he had to accomplish the next day. Schwab was to then number them in order of importance. The next day he was to work on priority number one until it was done, and then move to number two, and so on.

Occasionally he was to recheck his priorities and then continue on. Lee recommended that Schwab make this a daily habit.

That one idea turned the Bethlehem Steel Corporation—in just five years—into the biggest independent steel producer in the world. For that one idea, Lee was paid $25,000! Simple? Yes. Effective? Absolutely!

3. Track your boundaries. Ministry has a way of blurring boundaries. It's often hard to separate our call from our personal life. Usually the lines begin to blur, and we start to see them as one and the same. So choosing when to say yes and when to say no presents real challenges. On top of that, ministry is about people. People assume that those in ministry—paid and nonpaid—should serve them when-ever they need help or attention.

Knowing our purpose and tracking our priorities help us set boundaries. They make it possible for us to say no or yes when it's appropriate without feeling guilty. For example, from the start of my ministry I decided I would not attend every committee meeting and church gathering. My job was to ensure that all of those meetings had the best leadership available. But I didn't and don't attend the overwhelming majority of them. Those kinds of boundaries keep me fresh for ministry and in the race for the long haul.

4. Track "the ball." A few years ago a reporter from the East Coast visited our church to review one of our worship services. We had no idea he had been with us until the magazine editors called a few months later to ask if they could take a picture of one of the pastors. They explained that their publication would be featuring us, along with several other Valley churches. I was the only pastor available at the time, so I posed for the picture and anxiously waited for the magazine to appear.

The article was not very flattering. While the writer gave

us an overall high score, he had very few nice things to say about our worship service. In fact, after reading his review I was totally embarrassed (and sick that my big smiling face was so prominent). After stewing on the article for several days, I realized that everything he said was true. We had lost our edge. The quality was slipping. And I determined the reason for it was that we had too many irons in the fire. We had lost sight of the ball.

So I met with the performing arts team and handed each one of them an orange golf ball. I told them we needed to keep our eye on the ball and that that ball is worship. Anything that takes our focus away from the ball needed to be reevaluated. We still find ourselves, due to the demands of ministry, flying from one event to another. So every once in a while we have to take out the orange ball to refocus ourselves, our time, our priorities, and our mission.

Fired-Up or Burned-Out?

Two paddleboats left Memphis about the same time, headed down the Mississippi River to New Orleans. As they traveled side by side one of the sailors remarked to a sailor on the other boat about how slow his boat was going. Soon the good-natured teasing turned into a challenge. And the race was on. The competition grew fierce as the two boats headed down the river.

Eventually one of the boats fell behind. It didn't have enough fuel. Race speed used it up too quickly. So to make the ship go faster, the crew started throwing the boat's cargo into the coal furnace. Sure enough, the boat began to pick up speed. They threw more cargo into the furnace. As a result, they won the race. Unfortunately, they burned their entire cargo. They were so caught up in the urgent—in winning the race—that they lost sight of the important—delivering their goods.

For sprinters, time is crucial. In a marathon, pacing and finishing, not time, are most important (at least for those of us who don't run marathons to earn our livelihoods). If the clock becomes the guiding force, a runner can go too fast and burn out before finishing the race. So many marathoners focus on the compass—on the finish line— and see the clock as secondary.

The same holds true for the ministry marathon. When we allow the urgent to overwhelm us, we begin to lose sight of what really matters and burn up in the process. Keeping our purpose, priorities, boundaries, and mission in mind helps us better manage our time. It also helps us manage the inevitable "urgents" that ministry often produces.

Tracking our time has much to say as well about doing a better job of caring for our hearts, which is perhaps the most important facet of running the ministry marathon.

8 miles

*T*raining is principally
an act of faith.
—Frans Stamfl,
Austrian-born
professional coach

MINISTRY LAKE MARATHO
Start/Finish

Training Tip #6
Hone Your Heart

Above all else, guard your heart,
for it is the wellspring of life.
—Proverbs 4:23 NIV

I've worked here for the past ten years. Same chair, same gray metal desk, same family picture in the same wooden frame. I really should have a new family picture taken. But who has the time? When I started my job here as the church secretary—executive to the pastor, I like to call myself—I loved it. The excitement of ministry, the satisfaction of programs that run well, and seeing new people join the church made my part in it all seem worthwhile and important.

But lately the fizz has gone out of the work. My heart doesn't pound with anticipation before launching into a new ministry idea like it used to. Lately I feel overwhelmed, overworked, and as if I'm on my way to the funny farm.

I usually arrive at work at 8:00 a.m. and check the messages first thing. Pastor doesn't usually get here until 9:00 or so, but that's fine by me. I used to use that

hour for my personal devotional time, but that ended about three years ago. Now that hour is taken up with returning phone calls, filing, and general morning business. Occasionally I manage to make a pot of coffee before Pastor arrives, but that, like my devotions, has taken a backseat to the other stuff.

I guess you could say I'm a jack-of-all-trades in this office. I am the writer of bulletins, the typer of sermons (Pastor never did learn to type), the filer of music and other assorted documents, and oftentimes the janitor. Our small church has experienced modest growth over the past few years, but the general fund doesn't reflect it. That means no extra money for extra help. No extra money for better equipment.

Okay. That's not entirely true. The council did vote to get an upgraded copy machine so that the bulletins could actually be read. I guess they got tired of the long black stripes and little black dots that have decorated the bulletins the last ten years. But along with the new copy machine came the "understanding" that I would make the bulletins look "flashier." So the machine really was a mixed blessing. Bulletin-making takes a large chunk of one whole day. And then getting music ready for the choir (the director works only part-time and has no time to get the music ready for rehearsal) takes a good deal of time as well.

I guess what I'm trying to say is that when I hired on for this job, the work of ministry had much more meaning for me than it does now. It was about reaching people for the Lord. It was about helping people grow in faith. I don't feel that way anymore. Now it is just another job, with long hours and little pay. Somehow God is supposed to be at the heart of this job, but not anymore.

How did I get to this point? It seems the chaos slowly creeps in and catches you unaware, and before you know it, ministry becomes a rat race. I need to find the heart of ministry. But quite honestly, I'm not sure how.

I come from a family with a history of heart disease. My grandpa Wright died at the age of fifty-five from his third heart attack. In March of 1998, my dad suffered a

> **Training Log**: *April 18.*
>
> *Ran two hours.*
> *Spent a good deal of time praying.*
> *Actually feel pretty good.*

major heart attack, his fourteenth in the last twenty-three years. The first one hit him when he was thirty-eight years old. I've seen the toll it's taken on his life, and I have no desire to go through that kind of stuff. So I'm motivated to care for my heart. My goal is to die healthy. I exercise regularly, I try to eat right, and I try to keep the stress managed.

The Bible continually encourages us to hone our hearts. But in so doing, it looks at the heart not simply as a physical organ, but as the seat of our thoughts and emotions. Researchers now tell us that keeping our hearts healthy takes more than exercise and proper diet. We also need to attend to the spiritual dimensions of the heart as well.

Spiritually Flabby

A man made an appointment to see his pastor. The man explained that he was feeling depressed—that his life lacked energy. The pastor asked if he exercised regularly. It turned out that the man was a workout-aholic. He spent two hours a day running, and on three of those days, he also spent thirty minutes at the club doing strength training. In addition, he played racquetball three times a week and tennis once or twice a week. Yet he still had little energy.

As they continued to talk the man finally made a telling confession. He said, "I think I know what the problem is. I'm physically fit, but I'm spiritually flabby."

The last people in the world we'd expect to be spiritually flabby are ministry people. Our lives are lived in the spiritual arena every day. We deal with spiritual matters, study spiritual insights, share those insights with others, and invest our lives into people. But many of us in ministry, if pushed, would have to admit that often spirituality is our job, not our experience. We can easily neglect our own spiritual health, and like the man above, become spiritually flabby. We can get so caught up in the business of spirituality that we miss out on its power in our own lives and end up feeling numb and tired.

My Personal Experience

As I mentioned earlier, during the writing of this book I found myself in a funk. Many factors contributed to it. Our church had been in the process of moving from one campus to another. It was a time filled with lots of excitement but also lots of chaos. Everything, it seemed, was in turmoil. The staff had been agitated. Our people were anxious. The growth of the ministry was driving us out of our comfort zone. And on top of that, I turned forty!

For the first time in fifteen years, ministry had not been fun. I felt empty inside, passionless, and at times even questioned my ability to get the job done. Occasionally the will to retire (at age forty) almost overwhelmed the desire to keep at it.

Thankfully, the training tips in this book kept me in the race. I've discovered, however, that honing the heart rises above all the other tips. Keeping my heart fit has enabled me to hang in there and trudge through a low time in life and ministry.

In training for the Walt Disney World marathon, I learned the importance of hydrating (drinking plenty of fluids) and carbo-loading (eating energy foods) before and during the run. Such actions give runners the reserves they need when they feel energy waning with miles yet to go. In the marathon of ministry, honing the heart does the same thing. Like putting money in the bank for a rainy day, honing our hearts helps store up reserves for those times when we feel drained and unable to go on.

The following training plan can help you build a fit heart:

1. Proper warm-up. Every good training program begins with warming up. When we take time to warm up the heart, we prepare it for the exercise we're about to give it. A proper warm-up keeps us from injuring ourselves. Prayer is a great warm-up exercise for the heart. It opens us up to God and keeps us spiritually limber.

A small town in the country had all the necessary institutions: a hospital, a courthouse, a church, and a cemetery. It also had the necessary services: tailors, shoemakers, carpenters, and masons. The one thing the little town didn't have, however, was a watchmaker.

Over the years many of the town's clocks became so inaccurate that several of the owners decided to ignore them. Others maintained their clocks and wound them every day even though they knew the time was no longer accurate.

One day a watchmaker came to town, and all of the people rushed their clocks over to him. But the only clocks he could repair were those that had been wound every day. The abandoned clocks had grown too rusty; the parts no longer moved.

Prayer keeps our hearts supple. Time alone talking with and listening to God strengthens the heart by making it pliable. A heart without prayer eventually hardens and shrivels up.

Many of us in ministry often make the fatal mistake of believing that we don't need personal devotional time. We see our sermon preparation or Bible studies or worship leadership as meeting that need. But there's a huge difference between studying about or talking about God and actually spending intimate, personal time with God. Healthy hearts discipline themselves to warm up daily with an inspiring dose of prayer.

2. Strength training. Strength training is the hot new button for fitness experts. They tell us that to keep our bones and bodies strong we need twenty to thirty minutes of strength training two or three times per week. The point of strength training is to work the muscles to the point of exhaustion. As the muscle rests and then works to exhaustion on a regular basis it grows stronger.

The heart also needs strength training—every day. Training it on the Word of God will keep it strong and healthy. Again, reading God's Word devotionally is different from studying it for the purpose of a class or sermon. Strength training on God's Word builds a stronger heart by inviting the Spirit to internalize and personalize what God is saying to us.

I've found the *One Year Bible* (Wheaton, Ill.: Tyndale House Publishers, 1985) to be extremely helpful in keeping me motivated to strengthen my heart every day. In ten minutes a day for a year I can read through the Bible. I don't try to figure out the meaning of a verse or exegete a verb. I simply read it devotionally and allow it to shape my thoughts and heart.

3. Aerobics. Getting one's heart rate up for an extended period of time is crucial for heart health. Running, swimming, walking, biking, and other aerobic sports help us build a strong physical heart.

Some doctors say that laughter is the aerobic workout for the soul. Norman Cousins said that laughter is internal jogging. Laughter reduces tension, massages the heart, stimulates blood circulation, increases the body's natural painkillers, lowers stress, and helps the lungs breathe easier. Laughter also enhances relationships and is a key ingredient for a more satisfying marriage. The Bible tells us that a cheerful heart is good medicine. Few things in life make us feel better or healthier than a good, deep laugh. Laughter is God's gift that lightens the soul and keeps the heart energized. Everybody, particularly those of us running the marathon of ministry, need a strong dose of laughter every day.

4. Stretching and cooling down. Stretching keeps us limber and prevents injuries. It also enables us to cool down after a good, intensive workout. As I've mentioned before, without rest our exercise actually becomes counterproductive.

Weekly worship provides the cool down and stretching period that we need. It enables us to slow down and heal. It refreshes us and replenishes our strength.

The leader of a safari was in a hurry to get to his destination. He kept pushing the team as hard as he could. On the third day of the journey he was up early and ready to go. He noticed that his workers, however, were sitting on their haunches. No matter what he did, he couldn't get them to move or break camp. So he asked his assistant what was going on. The assistant said very simply, "They're waiting for their souls to catch up to their bodies."

The Bible tells us that in quietness and trust shall be our strength; that those who wait on the Lord will renew their strength. Worship gives us the opportunity to slow down and allow God to stretch out sore muscles and recharge the batteries. Those of us who lead worship may need to find other worship opportunities where we can worship rather than lead, for worship is an essential part of honing the heart.

One other aspect of honing the heart deserves special attention—integrity.

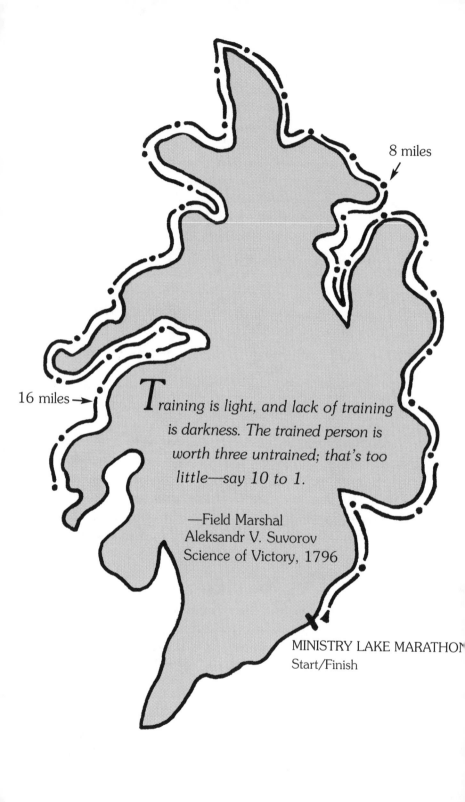

8 miles

16 miles →

*T*raining is light, and lack of training is darkness. The trained person is worth three untrained; that's too little—say 10 to 1.

—Field Marshal
Aleksandr V. Suvorov
Science of Victory, 1796

MINISTRY LAKE MARATHON
Start/Finish

Training Tip #7
Own Up to Others

> Whoever walks in integrity walks securely,
> but whoever follows perverse ways will be found out.
> —Proverbs 10:9 NRSV

They had her surrounded. Eight of the most intimidating people she had ever known. Their powdered wigs and long black robes set an eerie mood in the dark paneled boardroom. Through the dim lights she could see the anger glowing from their eyes. And she could feel their gazes on her like a slap of wind on a stormy night. The church council had called this meeting late at night to exact their judgment on her for what they claimed were "major character flaws." Needless to say, she was frightened.

She stood in the center of their circle, and as she slowly turned and met their gazes the allegations were hurled at her.

"You're a fraud!"

"You're a liar!"

"You have broken the rules!"

Tears began streaming down her face. Her legs trembled with the weight of her pain. Were they right? Had her life spun so out of control?

Then, out of the clouds of her doubts and fears, a strange beeping noise caught her attention. It grew louder and louder. Beep . . . beep . . . beep . . . the alarm clock. She bolted upright in her bed at once, relieved that the church council meeting had been a dream, and yet worried that the dream might be a subconscious reality check.

Anna had been the volunteer Women's Ministry director at the church in her hometown for many years, and she loved every aspect of the position. But lately she felt that she was losing her edge—largely because of her personal life.

She carried a secret that no one could ever know. As a result, she found herself constantly trying to cover her tracks. Little white lies had become commonplace. She felt awful, ashamed, unhappy, and alone. And she sensed a brick wall building between her and the Lord.

As Anna stood in front of the mirror that morning the realization of what she had become hit her square in the face. She didn't like her reflection anymore. She didn't like what she had become. She felt ugly inside. "What are you gonna do, Anna?" she asked her reflection. And that morning, with tears in her eyes, she slowly walked to the phone, lifted the receiver, and decided to make the hardest phone call of her life.

She heard the ringing on the other end of the line. One ring . . . two rings . . . "Hello, this is Pastor Martinez." She gulped, took a deep breath, and said, "Hi, Pastor, this is Anna. I need some help." And with that she emitted a sigh of relief. The first and hardest step toward home had been taken. She was on her way.

86

A young girl was walking around a toy store when she noticed a big clown-punching balloon. She looked at it for a moment and then hit it in the nose. The

Training Log: January 18.

Ran the San Diego Marathon in exactly 4:50:39.

clown fell over and then popped right back up again. It caught the little girl by surprise. So she hit the clown again, and again the clown fell on its back only to pop up once more. This went on for several minutes when the young girl's dad, who had been watching her, asked, "Honey, why do you think the clown comes back up when you knock him down?"

His daughter thought a moment and replied, "I don't know. I guess it's because he's standing up on the inside."

Keeping pace in the marathon of ministry certainly requires skill and ability. But more important than skill and ability is character—being a person who consistently stands up on the inside. We live in a society today that longs for leaders of character—leaders who can be counted on, people of integrity, people who do stand up on the inside.

Dwight L. Moody, one of the great preachers of the nineteenth century, said that character is "what you are in the dark." Character is the way we live, act, and respond when we don't think anyone is looking. It is the heart and soul of who we are. Character is a matter of the heart. As one writer put it, when God measures people, God puts the tape measure around their hearts, not their heads.

In Matthew 12:33-35 Jesus reminds us that what we treasure in our hearts—the thoughts, values, and insights stored there—shapes our character. When certain occasions arise we draw from that treasure, and what we bring out—the character traits—molds our decisions, actions, and responses. Those traits, in turn, determine the quality of our lives and the quality of our ministries. In other words, character matters, because character will either make or break us. It will either make or break our ministries. Horace Greeley put it this way: "Fame is a vapor; popularity an accident. Riches take wings. . . . Only one thing endures. Character."

Jesus upholds the value of character because he knows that a healthy, consistent character leads to wholeness. It energizes us with joy and contentment. It empowers us with the freedom of knowing that we don't have anything to hide. It enables us to look into the mirror each day and feel good about what we see. Integrity keeps us energized for the long haul of ministry.

A lack of integrity, on the other hand, robs us of joy. It fills us with shame, guilt, and fear. It keeps us from running at full speed. It holds us back from being the leaders God called us to be. And, worst of all, character scandals can destroy us, our ministries, and the people we serve.

Character Matters

As stories about character lapses involving political, business, entertainment, and religious leaders dominate the headlines, the issue of character becomes increasingly important particularly for Christian leaders, whether paid or nonpaid. People not only want to hear what we have to say, they also want to see what we believe in how we live our lives. They long for authentic leaders who really believe what they preach.

Walt Kallestad, senior pastor of Community Church of

Joy, had an experience that proves the point. While wait-ing to pay for a car wash, he picked up a couple of music tapes. He paid the bill and walked out to his car. As he looked over the receipt he saw that he had been under-charged. So he went back inside and told the cashier that he hadn't been charged enough. She looked him in the eye and said, "I know. I visited your church last Sunday, and I wanted to see if you're an honest man."

Integrity. Character. Standing up on the inside. Owning up to others. Building a heart of integrity is crucial in a time when people long for authentic leaders.

Forging a Healthy Character

Many of the training tips already outlined in this book can help us to nurture integrity. Staying intimate with Jesus, spending time in worship and devotions, setting boundaries, and so on help develop consistency in charac-ter. A few other integrity tips may also prove helpful.

1. Watch what you eat. A Native American legend is told of the son of a great chief who, though strong and handsome, did not exhibit the same leadership qualities as his dad. Whereas people admired the chief, they had doubts about his son. And the son knew it. He wanted to be like his dad, but he just wasn't wired the same way.

One day he went to his dad and poured out his heart. He shared his dreams of how he wanted to be a great leader and how those dreams were continually squelched by his fears.

His father listened quietly and then said, "Son, when I was your age, I had the same struggles. It was like two dogs warring within me. The good dog made me feel like

I could do anything. The bad dog made me feel like a failure. It tried to convince me that I had nothing to offer. They seemed to be fighting within me all the time."

The son immediately lit up. "Father, that's exactly how I feel. But how can I make sure the good dog wins out?"

"The answer is simple, my son. The dog who wins is the one you feed the most."

As Jesus reminds us, character is forged in the depths of our hearts. So our character is dependent on what we feed the heart. That's why it's important to nourish our hearts on those things that build and stimulate integrity.

2. Own up to others. More often than not, those who experience character lapses are those with little or no connections to others. Leaders serious about integrity surround themselves with those who can hold them accountable. Whether it's a staff person, a good friend, a counselor, or a church board, people who stand up on the inside own up to others. Accountability keeps them honest.

3. Be faithful in the small things. I read an article sometime ago that talked about the relationship between the way people play golf and the way they conduct business. Fifty-five percent of the four hundred executives surveyed for the article admitted that they cheated at golf at least once a week. Their offenses included taking an extra tee shot, failing to count a missed tap-in, undercounting the number of strokes, and secretly producing a fresh ball while pretending to look for one lost in the woods. One-third of those who confessed to cheating on the golf course also admitted to cheating on the job.

Being faithful in the small things builds the foundation for being faithful in the large things. Leaders of integrity look for consistency in all areas of their lives.

4. Avoid compromising situations. Churches all across the country are littered with the broken lives of those

who've been hurt by leaders who didn't heed this advice. Whether out of naïveté, ignorance, or the belief that they wouldn't fall, many ministry people have allowed themselves to be ruined by situations they should never have been in in the first place: after-hours counseling sessions with a person of the opposite sex; a "harmless" dinner with a volunteer while one's spouse is out of town; a church entertainment budget with no checks and balances; a weak, incompetent board with no accountability responsibility for a strong pastor; and the list goes on and on.

Leaders who value their integrity view ministry with a healthy sense of paranoia; they constantly look out for compromising situations that can ruin them, their ministries, their families, and bring embarrassment to the church.

Flying High in the Marathon of Ministry

A little boy was walking through a park one day when he noticed a man selling balloons. The little boy didn't have any money, so he mentally chose the balloon he would buy if he did have the money. He chose a big, bright, blue one.

As he stood dreaming about the balloon a little girl approached the balloon vendor and purchased the big, bright, blue balloon. The little boy looked on sadly as the girl took the balloon, played with it for awhile, and then let it go. He watched as the balloon floated higher and higher into the air.

Finally, the boy walked over to the vendor and asked, "Which of these balloons is the cheapest?" The vendor showed him a gray one and offered it to him for free.

Before taking it the boy asked, "Mister, will this balloon go just as high as the pretty blue one if I let it go?" The vendor replied, "Sure it will. You see, it's not what's on the outside of a balloon that determines how high it will go, but what's on the inside."

The same holds true for the marathon of ministry. Skills, training, long hours, serving as a volunteer, and great sermons help build a great ministry, but what's happening inside—what's happening in our hearts—determines the quality, the effectiveness, and the longevity of our work. For character enables us to fly high as we run the distance, which leads us to our final training tip—nurturing our nature.

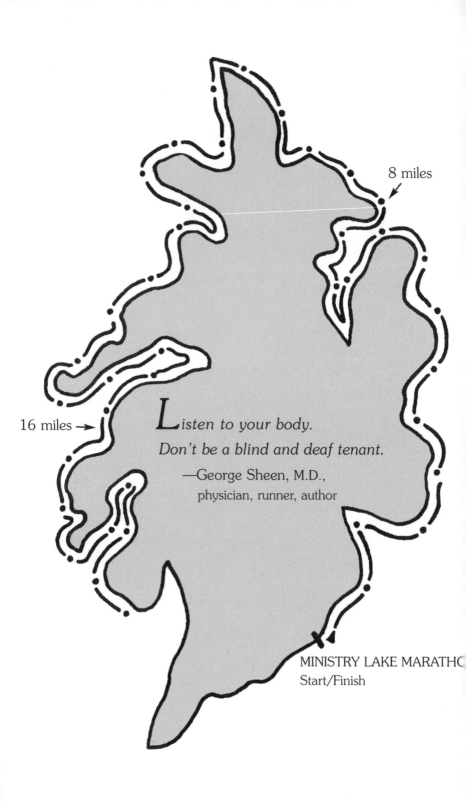

8 miles

16 miles →

*L*isten *to your body.*
Don't be a blind and deaf tenant.
—George Sheen, M.D.,
  physician, runner, author

MINISTRY LAKE MARATHON
Start/Finish

Training Tip #8
Nurture Your Nature

When I look at your heavens, the work of your
fingers, the moon and the stars that you have
established; what are human beings that you are
mindful of them, mortals that you care for them?
Yet you have made them a little lower than God,
and crowned them with glory and honor.
—Psalm 8:3-5 NRSV

*It had been a long, long winter for John and Jenny.
They found themselves desperately needing to find
new employment before they lost their house and
everything they owned. The church where they had
previously served had to let them and several other
employees go. The congregation had no other choice;
financial difficulties almost forced the members to
close the doors of the church. That was four months
ago, and John and Jenny were scared.*

After months of growing debt, harassing phone calls

from creditors, and general family depression, things started to take a turn for the better, or so they thought. A church in Phoenix had an opening for an associate pastor. And as coincidence would have it, the former associate's wife had been the wedding coordinator, so there was a place for Jenny, too. John and Jenny were thrilled. Well, maybe thrilled wasn't exactly the word. They were happy. Well, not happy, either. They were desperate.

So with little prayer and no counsel from friends or family, they packed up their kids and drove several thousand miles to their new home. John and Jenny put on happy faces and began the task of trying to fit into a situation where they didn't necessarily belong. They worked diligently to become friends with those around them. They threw themselves into special projects and committees. But instead of fitting in, they felt increasingly alone.

Pretty soon they found themselves tired and depressed. Jenny knew almost nothing about coordinating weddings. She often felt confused and in way over her head. And she didn't really enjoy it anyway. John, used to being in control of his own areas of ministry, found himself less and less enthused about the job because of all of the bureaucracy and hand-tying. The two of them moved from morning until night like automatons with little feeling or emotion, simply trying to make it through the day.

They knew the whole charade would one day come tumbling down on them. And it came sooner than expected. The senior pastor showed up in John's office early one morning for a chat. John deeply admired and respected the senior pastor. But their ideas on ministry often clashed. John didn't have the commitment to the particular ministry vision that Pastor Phelps had, and they both knew it. John knew that something would have to change.

Later that day, after his meeting with Pastor Phelps,

John sat alone pondering where he and Jenny had gone wrong. He thought back to the day when they were told they were out of a job. The anger and hurt. And he thought about the day when they were hired for this new job. At the time it had seemed like a miracle. Surely it was a gift from God. And they needed the job, not to mention the income, didn't they? But now Pastor Phelps had him thinking about the whole issue of and meaning of "the call," John's own personal call. What exactly was God's call on his life?

Successful runners know themselves well. They know their strengths and weaknesses, their limitations and possibilities. They begin their quest for success by evaluating themselves. For instance, they determine the kind of shape they're in and carefully and slowly build up their endurance. They look at the structure of their body, particularly their feet. Do they overpronate? If so, they could injure themselves. They may need shoes that adjust for the problem, or even orthotics to correct the situation. What do the arches of their feet look like? If they have high arches, the runners may battle shin splints. That happened to me. When I got back into running, I developed very sore shins. My sports doctor saw that I had high arches, so he prescribed orthotics, which helped tremendously.

> **Training Log: July 10.**
>
> *Ran an hour and a half but had to walk the last thirty minutes. I overheated.*

Once on the road, successful runners listen to their bodies. They learn to determine how much pounding they can take. I find I can only run three days a week. More than that, and my shins get sore. As runners experience twinges of pain they have to consider whether or not the pain is serious or just part of the routine of running. If they're feeling sluggish over a period of weeks, they have to find out why. Maybe they're overdoing it and not getting enough rest. I remember one particular run when the temperature was warmer than I had expected. I started overheating. Thankfully, I listened to my body, started walking, and drank water every chance I could. I had suffered the early stages of heat stroke. Had I not listened to my body I could have become very sick, or even worse.

The point is that successful runners know themselves well, they listen to their bodies as they exercise, and they continually nurture and build on their strengths.

The marathon of ministry is no different. To run it successfully, we need to know who we are so that we can nurture our strengths and abilities. Nurturing the following areas of our lives will enable us to hang in there during the ministry run.

1. Nurture your personality. I work with a very special senior pastor whose ability to dream is unsurpassed. Walt Kallestad has a way of seeing the best in people and drawing it out. As one of our staff members once said, "Walt can tell you where to go, and you want to go there." He builds relationships easily by putting people at ease with his winsome smile. My mother-in-law, upon first meeting him, said, "He looked me right in the eyes, and I felt like I had known him all of my life."

When I first arrived at Community Church of Joy, as a seminary student, I was deeply impressed by Walt. As one studying to be a pastor, I looked up to him as a person I wanted to emulate. In fact, I thought I had to be just like Walt. But as our relationship developed over the years, I found that I couldn't do it. While we have some personality traits in common, for the most part we're quite different from each other. I eventually found myself frustrated because I couldn't be like him. I'm introverted whereas he's extroverted. I love to spend my time in the office preparing for a sermon, a class, or a lecture. Walt prefers to be out with people. I'm more difficult to get to know than is Walt, at least initially.

Eventually I discovered that I can't be like Walt because God has wired me differently. I have a different kind of personality. I have strengths Walt doesn't have. He has strengths I don't have. And as I discovered my strengths and personality I felt more comfortable with myself and, as a result, could build on my strengths and work on my weaknesses. Looking back, that discovery was one of the most freeing of my early ministry.

A man who had lived on a farm all of his life began to tire of it. He longed for something new. Every day he found something about his home to criticize. Finally, he decided to sell it. So he called a real estate agent and put the farm on the market.

The real estate agent wrote a beautiful description of the farm. The ad talked about the ideal location, the modern equipment, the healthy livestock, the fertile ground, and so on. After the farmer read it, he called up the real estate agent and said, "Hold everything. I've decided not to sell. I've been looking for a place like that all of my life."

While running the ministry marathon, it's easy to become critical of ourselves or compare ourselves to others. Because we may not feel that we measure up to others, we soon run out of steam and feel like giving up. Learning to enjoy who we are, however, can help us enjoy the run. So in order to stay in the race we need to assess and nurture our personality. Are you a detailed person or a dreamer? Introverted or extroverted? A saver or thrower? A thinker or a talker? Decisive or indecisive? Fact or feeling oriented? A peacemaker or confronter? A morning person or an evening person?

Knowing who we are and playing to our strengths keep us energized.

2. Nurture your gifts. Along with personality and

strengths, God's Spirit has given each of us significant spiritual gifts that we can use to further the work of the Kingdom. These gifts include teaching, evangelism, hospitality, mercy, giving, exhortation, administration, and leadership, to name a few. I don't believe we all have all of the gifts. I do believe, however, that all of us, whether we're ordained or not, have one or more of these "gifts of the Spirit." And when we use our gifts, we find ourselves energized over and over again.

In college, two teachers sensed in me the gift of evangelism. They both saw that God had gifted me with the ability to speak to people, particularly in large group settings, in ways that helped them connect with the gospel. The teachers' encouragement motivated me to develop that gift and learn all I could about being an effective speaker. My greatest joy in life comes when I'm speaking because I'm using the gifts God has given me.

Too many volunteers and paid staff people burn out because they aren't using their gifts. They serve in areas not suited to their gifts and find themselves quickly frustrated. When we discover our gifts and use them, we stay fresh and enthused for the whole race.

3. Nurture your call. I felt the call to ministry when I was in second grade. I remember watching my grandpa as he led a service at Bible camp. He invited people to come forward to the altar for prayer—to either renew their faith or receive Jesus for the first time (a bold concept for a Lutheran pastor!). I was so moved as hundreds of people came forward that I knew I wanted to have that kind of impact on people. That call has been the driving force of my life ever since.

Having been in ministry for a few years now, I know that the call is crucial. Sometimes that's all we have to hang on to when we hit the wall. The call pulls us through.

When we interview potential staff people, we always say to

them, "Don't come unless you can't stay away. If God hasn't called you to Joy, it will never work." The call is that important.

A few years ago I had the chance to see the Sistine chapel. The colors and pictures were breathtaking. That hasn't always been the case. Over the years grime built up on the ceiling, muting the colors. In fact, some "experts" criticized Michelangelo's choice of colors, calling them boring and unimaginative. But after a twelve-year restoration project the criticisms changed. Once the grime and grit was removed, the brilliance of his color choices was evident for all to see.

All too often we find our call marred by the soot and grime of ministry. Frustrations, criticisms, church battles, success, failure, weariness, and a host of other experiences can muddy it. If we're not careful, we can begin to question the call. Many have dropped out of the race for precisely that reason. Their call to ministry had been muted due to the grime of ministry life.

In those times we need to get away and let God's Spirit remove the gunk that clouds the call. During the frustrating year that I mentioned earlier, I prayed that God would give me the first love for mission that I had when I started. We all need those times of refreshing, renewal, and cleansing to keep us in the race. We need to nurture the call.

4. Nurture your passion. Without passion, nothing great happens. Passion is the fuel of life and mission. Passion is the deep-seated commitment in the pit of our stomach that consumes us. We'd rather do that one thing we're passionate about than eat or sleep. Passion enables us to endure the cross for the joy set before us. It keeps us in the race. Without it, we simply can't go on. I'm convinced that passion is the most important ingredient for running the marathon of ministry successfully. I'm also convinced that many of us in ministry, both paid and nonpaid, have lost the passion. That's why so many are dropping out of the race. What we need is a new dose of life-enhancing passion.

Several years ago my wife and I saw the Broadway musical *Les Misérables*. I was so moved by the experience that I read Victor Hugo's book, all fourteen hundred small-print pages of it.

Les Misérables tells the story of Jean Valjean, a decent man who spent nineteen years in prison for stealing a loaf of bread to feed his sister's starving family. Those nineteen years drained him of life and passion, turning him into the hardened criminal he was accused of being. When he was released from prison, he discovered that life on the outside was even more difficult than life on the inside. Because he was an ex-con, he couldn't get a job, buy food, or find a place to stay. He was continually ostracized by the community and harassed by the police.

Finally, near the end of his rope, Valjean found himself on the doorstep of the home of Bishop Myriel, a man known for his compassion. He invited Valjean in for dinner and offered him a place to sleep. During dinner Valjean noticed the expensive silverware, and a plan began to form in his mind. In the middle of the night he crept downstairs, grabbed the silverware, and ran. But he ran right into the police. He tried to convince them that the bishop had given him the silverware, but they didn't believe him. They dragged him back to the bishop's house to make their accusation. But when the bishop opened the door, he shocked them all. He looked at Valjean and said, "Ah, there you are. I'm glad to see you. You forgot to take these silver candlestands along with the silverware. They should get you several hundred francs." And with that, he dismissed the police.

Valjean was stunned. He didn't know what was happening. Then Bishop Myriel bent down and whispered something into Valjean's ear that changed Valjean forever.

"Don't forget that you promised me to use that silver to become an honest man."

Valjean had made no such promise and the bishop knew it. But he continued: "Jean Valjean, you no longer belong to evil but to good. I am giving your soul to God."

Victor Hugo writes that Jean Valjean was "dazzled by virtue." Those words of grace and love restored his dignity, his worth, and his passion, and gave him a new lease on life. And Jean Valjean did become a new man.

The key to restoring our passion is to be dazzled again and again by the virtue of Jesus. To experience his grace as it washes over us. To sit back and enjoy his love and words of kindness and belief in us. We also experience renewed passion when we see the changes that take place in people when they, too, are dazzled by the love of Christ. Nothing energizes us more quickly than seeing someone transformed as a result of our ministry. As ministers of the gospel, we need to pray that God would let us see the work God's doing from time to time so that we can rediscover our passion for mission and ministry.

Nurturing our personality, gifts, call, and passion will keep us in the marathon of ministry by filling us with new joy, confidence, energy, and enthusiasm.

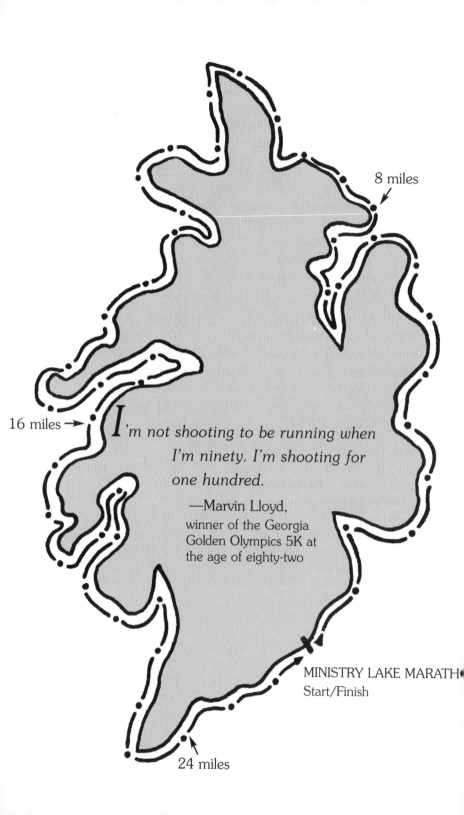

8 miles

16 miles →

I'm not shooting to be running when I'm ninety. I'm shooting for one hundred.

—Marvin Lloyd,
winner of the Georgia
Golden Olympics 5K at
the age of eighty-two

MINISTRY LAKE MARATHON
Start/Finish

24 miles

Run for the Finish Line

I have not yet *reached* my goal, and I am not perfect. But Christ has taken hold of me. So I keep on running and struggling to take hold of the prize. My friends, I don't feel that I have already arrived. But I forget what is behind, and I struggle for what is ahead. I run toward the goal, so that I can win the prize of being called to heaven.
—Philippians 3:12-14a CEV

Training Log: *March 3*

I'm setting my eyes on another marathon. Am I nuts?

After the San Diego Marathon, I headed back to the hotel. My son, Mike, was waiting for me, and after I showered, we decided to grab some lunch. As we rang for the elevator I sat down to rest my weary body. The elevator arrived and out popped a man wearing a San Diego

Marathon Finisher medal. He looked about fifty. I asked him how he did. He said he didn't run as well as he normally ran. He had to battle a flare-up of arthritis in his knee, so he ran a "slow" three-hour-and-forty-three-minute marathon. Mike glanced at me with a "Wow, Dad, he smoked you and he's injured and older" kind of look. The man went on to say that his goal was to become the first person to run two marathons on each continent in the world. He only had three marathons left to complete his dream, a dream he hoped to accomplish within the year. Before leaving, he said he ran the San Diego Marathon, arthritis and all, because it was his seventieth birthday.

That guy is in it for the long haul, and loving every minute of it. But he didn't do it simply by trying. He's trained for it, and that training has become a transformational lifestyle.

I hope the training tips in this book will give you that same kind of enthusiasm and energy as you run the marathon of ministry. God has called you to a significant work in life. It takes a lot of time and energy. But nothing offers more joy than knowing that God is using you to change lives.

I know that you want to stay in the race as long as possible and enjoy every moment of it. So keep on running! We'll meet at the finish line!